EVERYONE NEEDS
A MRS. BAILEY

By

Dr. William D. Sroufe
with Rachelle Chartrand

Akmaeon Publishing, LLC
309 Firkle Ferry Road, Ste. 209
Cumming, Georgia 30040

Copyediting: Martha Chaney
Cover Design: David Stanley
Back Cover Photo: Kim Rakes

Dedication

To my children
Emma, Mitchell, and Benjamin
I love you more than you will ever know.

This book is gratefully dedicated
to my 6th grade teacher
Mrs. Frances Bailey whose impact
cannot be measured in simple words.
Thank you.

Out of suffering have emerged the strongest souls;
The most massive characters are seared with scars.

Khalil Gibran

Acknowledgements

My father Ralph Sroufe

I miss you every day.

My brother Ralph Sroufe, Jr.

I miss you every day.

My grandfather William E. Greene

I miss you every day.

Nicole and Ladi Shehu

I love you.

Rachelle Chartrand

I am thankful for your muse.
You have been a voice in a thousand memories.

Table of Contents

*Some names and identifying details have been changed
to protect the privacy of individuals.*

Forward

While I was not surprised that Bill Sroufe was writing his first book, I was pleasantly surprised when he asked me to write the foreword for his third book: *Everyone Needs a Mrs. Bailey*. For years, I have known that Bill is in a unique cadre of educators who can somehow see a bigger picture, provide multiple ways to reach success, and develop a deep and compassionate connection to every learner.

I am frequently on the receiving end of Bill's phone calls on his way to and from work; often these calls are evening de-briefings after Bill has spent another fifteen-hour day on the job. During these conversations, Bill never ceases to amaze me with his utter devotion to making things better for kids. I have worked in education my entire adult life, and I can count on one hand the number of individuals who possess something—

not completely sure what it is—that sets them apart from all other educators whom I have met. Do not get me wrong, I have met and worked with some of the finest in the business. For instance, I look up to author Todd Whittaker in the way most five-year-old children revere the Easter Bunny or Santa Claus. Bill, however, is different. Bill is real, never misaligned in his mission to maximize opportunities for kids. Bill can see through almost anything, he can reason and admit when he is wrong, and he will die on the hill if he believes he is right. He is special—he may not know it, but he is a rare breed, and this world is a better place because of his story and who that story has helped him become. I have never met Mrs. Bailey, but the world owes her; kids owe her: she has ignited a passion and selflessness that has made countless lives better.

On a personal note, Bill is a fine husband, father, and friend. He will tell you how it is, whether you like it or not. He cares deeply about his family, his country, and his faith. After reading *Everyone Needs a Mrs. Bailey* for the third time, I no longer felt the sorrow for Bill that I found during my initial review; instead, I found a great deal of peace for and understanding of one person's ability to carry such a burden only to be convinced that the greatest revenge would be to live well—and, of course, ultimately, to forgive.

Bill has lived well; he has loved, both his own and others. Bill has given his heart and his soul to this most important work, and he has done so while remaining true to the reason this book even exists. Everyone does need a Mrs. Bailey. Everyone!

Brian Kitts
Educator

Preface

I have been many people in my nearly 49 years on this earth. In this book alone, I am a frightened and abused child, whose identity was stolen, whose dreams were put on hold; I am a survivor; I am a veteran, father, son, grandson, poet; and I am an educator. But aside from trying to be the best father I can be, of all the things that each of these represents, as I look ahead to when I shed this mortal coil, and my life is looked upon by someone else, the role I want to be most remembered for is an educator. I want to be regarded as someone who made a difference upon the piece of the world I have touched by having connected with the youth under my care. I have learned that what makes the difference, above all else, is just conversation.

Conversation is what connects us. Through it, we are able to open up to a much deeper level of understanding and compassion. Although I have been many people in my life, it was a simple conversation in the dingy hallway of a small town elementary school that was pivotal in me becoming the man I am today, and still contributes to the vision of the man I aspire to become. I have since discovered that sharing this simple conversation, and its impact on me, has the power to inspire others. I guess what author Patti Dingh says is true: The shortest distance between two people really is a story.

About a year ago, during a Region 6 superintendent meeting, the chairman, Dr. Jared Cotton, asked for volunteers to do an Ignite session at the May 2017 VASS (Virginia Association of School Superintendents) Conference. After no one volunteered, I said I would do it.

My journey to becoming the superintendent of Patrick County Public Schools in Stuart, Virginia, has not been an easy or predictable one, so I was not exactly sure what I would talk about. Offhand, I could not think of anything particularly "igniting" about my path. I thought long and hard about a topic, though, and decided I would talk about why I became an educator, and about the impact some teachers had on me along the way.

This was a tough decision as I had told some people about my childhood, but not many, and it caused me to look back and think about where I had been, how far I had come and where I was going. It made me realize how important one person, in particular, was to me. It made me think of my sixth grade teacher, Mrs. Frances Bailey.

When I found out Leland Melvin would also be speaking, I was thrilled. Leland Melvin, who is originally from Lynchburg, Va., is an engineer, former NFL player, and former NASA astronaut. He served on board the Space Shuttle *Atlantis* as a mission specialist on STS-122, and as mission specialist 1 on STS-129. Over the years, I have collected autographs from people who I believe changed the American landscape, including astronauts like Buzz Aldrin, Charlie Duke, John Glenn, Jim Lovell and Wally Schirra. Leland's book, *Chasing Space: An Astronaut's Story of Grit, Grace, and Second Chances*, had not yet been released for publication, so I was excited that when I registered for the conference, I was given a copy and would hopefully have the opportunity to get Leland to sign it.

Between sessions, as I was walking through the hotel lobby, I saw a man sitting by himself in a blue jumpsuit. I knew immediately it was Leland; so book in hand, I went up to him to ask for his autograph. He was a very gracious man, sitting by himself with his laptop open and working. He obliged my request and offered me a seat. He asked a little about me and I explained that I had done an Ignite session, a five-minute talk meant to have a great impact, to make a specific point. I told him that I had shared how I had moved 30- plus times before I was 30, and talked about the teachers who had influenced me, in particular, Mrs. Bailey. I went on to explain to Leland how Mrs. Bailey was a very special person from my youth and how exactly she changed my life.

He was very attentive to my story, and eventually got his laptop out right there in front of me. He proceeded to change his speech to include my story. It was just the greatest, most surreal moment.

After I did my session, many of the other superintendents had come up to me and said, "That was so powerful." I was really moved that my story could inspire others that way, but then during his speech, Leland said, "Dr. Sroufe *needed* a Mrs. Bailey. I also had a Mrs. Bailey…" I could not believe he mentioned me after our brief encounter. I thought to myself, "Wow, if Leland Melvin's story was similar to mine, how many others are there out there that also are?"

I realized, maybe my story *does* matter. Maybe it is not only worth sharing, but a necessity. This was the trigger for this book—if I could, in a brief encounter, grab Leland Melvin's attention, then maybe other people would listen to what I had to say.

There is a loneliness sometimes in this world, particularly if you grow up in a violent and unpredictable household because the fear of repercussions keeps you silent. I know as an educator, teacher, principal and superintendent, how important it is for children to have a voice—a voice of the future, a voice of hope, a voice for the weak, a voice for courage in knowing that every child matters; and the key to success in working with children is to set high expectations with compassion and understanding, while building relationships with them. Moreover, that dreams really do matter as they fuel hope and motivation.

In the first part of this book, I will be sharing my story. I am usually not open about my past, especially in such great detail. There is an embarrassment about it for me. Some of the things in this book I have only told very few people. I think I was so afraid and so ashamed for so long I just wanted to leave the past behind me. I had blocked many of the stories out, as those burdens are heavy to carry around.

Nevertheless, I am not afraid anymore. I am ready to put the burden down and allow others to help carry it. My hope is that by sharing my story, I will shine a light on the darkness many children are going through right under our noses, and to create a new level of compassion for that kid in our class we just do not connect with or who is misbehaving.

It is my hope that by sharing my story, I will inspire and help other adults look beyond the emotional luggage a kid carries. I also want to make sure children and teenagers know that no matter what happens to them it does not define who they are. As educators, parents and compassionate adults, we have the opportunity—no, we have the *responsibility* to help them understand and believe this. I must say here, it is not easy, but I can tell you it is worth it.

In the second part, I will be sharing some of my personal experiences as an educator—some wins and some losses when it came to creating relationships with youth—as well as exchanges and experiences I have witnessed along my journey.

Introduction

As I write this story, I have thought how it seems disjointed where usually stories of someone's childhood flow, with highlights of events weaving together throughout their life. There are some happy stories and some unhappy stories.

This is probably the most simplified definition of life there might be. I realized that with my childhood, there were not any highlights, there were not any dreams fulfilled, or outwardly, happy moments celebrated.

Do not get me wrong; I have fond memories of my grandparents and some childhood friends, but I can find nothing in my memory that is not overshadowed by the dark events in my life. There is a seediness to my story—a story of filth, neglect, and abuse. I may come across as ungrateful for my life, but I am not. I know that what happened to me, the experiences, helped shape me; I am who I am, in part because of those experiences.

Therefore, I guess that is what my childhood was—one event after another until I stepped away onto a new path. I wrote a poem once and one of the lines reads:

"… once before today, on a roadmap I have drawn, I escaped to do a song, and I ended up telling a story."

This is my story.

Prologue

My story actually begins before I was born, in a Peoples Drug Mart in the Hilltop area of Virginia Beach, Virginia, in 1962. My mother, Karen Ann Greene, 15, was working the soda fountain when my father, Ralph Edwin Sroufe, 16, sauntered in. My mother was a true beach girl, with her blond hair and tan skin. She looked like Farrah Fawcett; he looked like Bob Newhart—not exactly a match made in Hollywood. However, for some reason, he was able to sweep her off her feet.

The relationship started as casual. They dated on and off until they finally married—well, *eloped*, in Elizabeth City, NC, on April 25, 1965.

I remember my father telling me the story about how he told my grandfather about the secret nuptials:

"We came back from North Carolina to your grandparents' house in Wolf Snare (an area of Virginia Beach). I was a little afraid of telling your grandfather that your mother and I had just eloped. However, we went into the house, and I just spit it out. I told him what we did."

"Karen and I just eloped. In Elizabeth City. We're married," my father had said.

Apparently, my grandfather said, "You know what I am going to do?"

My father sat there in fear.

My grandfather finally put him out of his misery. "I'm gonna take you to dinner," he said.

My father sighed in relief.

Perhaps he would not have if he had known what the next decade of his life would be like.

Part I

My Birth

According to my birth certificate, I came into this world at exactly 8:28 PM on December 12th, 1968.

It was a Thursday.

As a rule, I don't usually believe in things like astrology or numerology or any other -ology that tries to assign a deeper meaning to the mundane, but I do think it is interesting that Thursday is named after the planet Jupiter, which supposedly symbolizes happiness and optimism; and Thursday's "children" are supposed to be jovial, often to the point of self-deception. This would definitely describe at least the first few years of my life.

Jupiter is also the teaching planet and children born on a Thursday often have a special insight to share with the world, which I hope is what this book will provide. Therefore, perhaps the mundane is more meaningful than I thought. However, back to my birth:

My father tells the story of the day I was born; he sat on the back steps of the Mary Immaculate Hospital with the head nun, a priest, Father David Walsh, who was also my godfather, and another nun, and passed around a fifth of bourbon toasting my birth.

As per my baby book inscriptions, my father's first words when I was born were, "Well, great! A son!"

My mother's were, "I don't believe it."

I am not sure exactly what it was she did not believe.

I weighed 7lbs 6.5oz and measured 21 inches, which was about average for babies born in America in the sixties, but for some reason, my mother claims I was a big baby. Apparently, she even thought she was going to have twins. The night I was born, while she was lying in her hospital bed half-asleep, she remembers faintly overhearing people talking about twins in the distance. My mother popped up and called the nurse in to ask if she had somehow unknowingly given birth to *two* babies. She had not; it was the woman in the room next to her.

She also said I was a whiny baby.

Although I was born in Newport News, VA, we lived in Hampton, VA, on Queen Street. My father was a pastor at Tyler Memorial Methodist Church, while my mother stayed home to take care of us. By us, I mean my older sister, Lisa Karen Sroufe, who was born on January 30, 1966, and me. My younger brother, Ralph E. Sroufe, Jr. would join us on December 16, 1972. I would love to say I remember my siblings fondly, but I really do not remember much of them growing up at all—neither good or bad.

Married

My first real memory of my parents is of them having an argument. I was very young at the time, barely four years old, so it appeared to me in snippets, which were later put together when the event was explained to me in more detail. However, the emotion of the event, I will never forget.

We were now living in Front Royal, VA, where my father was a Methodist minister at Riverton Methodist Church and my mother was a homemaker. My father was shaking his hands at her, but I do not recall why. He was only about 5'5" and 115lbs, but I remember him taking up a whole lot of space and energy with his anger.

My older sister was hiding in her room, my brother was crying in the background and I was just staring at my father. Watching him so upset was extremely upsetting for me, yet I could not take my eyes off him. Until, all of a sudden, his college ring came off his finger and sailed across the living room into our saltwater aquarium, shattering it.

I remember the yelling.

I remember the chaos.

I remember putting the broken pieces in the trunk of the car.

I remember the dead fish.

I remember it being the beginning of the end for my parents.

~~~~~~

Both my parents drank, which, of course, contributed to the arguing, although at such a young age, I did not yet make the connection. In fact, like many children, I wanted to be like my parents and modeled their behavior, even the bad habits.

One time, my father was mowing the grass while my sister and I sat on the front steps watching him. Brushing the sweat from his brow, he sent us inside to get him a beer. We must have been taking a long time because eventually, he came in to see what we were doing.

Not being able to find us inside, he checked the backyard: Nada. He came around the corner of the house to find us sitting there, cool as cucumbers, each drinking a Budweiser tall boy. He stopped at the corner and just stared.

After a moment, I began to take another drink, and he asked, "What are you doing?"

"Drinking a beer," I answered.

"Well maybe you and Lisa need something different to drink other than beer," he said. "Why don't you give me those and go inside and get something different?"

He gathered the cans, and Lisa and I went inside for something else to drink.

That was it for me and drinking for a long while, but it was not for my father.

The tension in the house worsened when the Methodist church asked my father to resign. His alcohol problem had become apparent to everyone, which is not the best reputation for a pastor to have, but it was also affecting his job. He later told me he had actually been missing weddings and funerals he was supposed to be officiating. The church elders would find him in bars; it did not take long for that to be the end of his liturgical career.

My father later explained to me that he had been angry with God; that there had been a young boy in his congregation who had leukemia. My father pleaded with God, begged him to allow this precious, little boy to live. However, God took him anyway.

This devastated my father, and although he never said it, I think his faith was shattered by the tragedy and lost for many years to come.

Without a congregation to lead, we subsequently moved back to Virginia Beach. I was sad to leave our home in Front Royal. Perhaps on some energetic level only children can feel, I sensed the end was near, but even more so, I was upset to go because I loved my bedroom. My father had taken the time to paint it carefully in stars and stripes. All I remember is standing in the doorway watching him work on it as if he were Michelangelo painting the Sistine Chapel, and then seeing it when it was done. With all the multiple colors and patterns, I was in awe.

Our house was small and the tension was thick, but I remember feeling secure in my room. One of the first places we lived in Virginia Beach was in the London Bridge Apartments. As I look back I know, I can recognize a psychological pattern to some of my behaviors that began in that home and would continue for years. I was barely five years old but sensing that my parents were not getting along, I began to do chores without being asked, trying to find ways to help around the house wherever and whenever I could. Mostly, I think my motivation was due to my father's obsession with cleanliness, and my mother's inability to meet his expectations. I guess I thought if I could keep the house clean, they would not fight.

There was one time I was trying to vacuum, and succeeded in doing a superb job, but could not pull the cord out of the socket. Therefore, I did what any preschooler would do; I used my mouth to pull it out, biting the cord in the process. If I close my eyes, I can still see the flashes of light from the electricity running through my body. I remember the electricity tossed my body, leaving an impression on the hollow door I flew into. The power of the thrust actually saved my life as the cord was subsequently pulled out of the wall. I still have the scar.

Along with trying to help around the house and keep things perfect, I guess I was also garnering attention as my parents' marriage was crumbling. One evening, I remember my sister and I were playing with a lighter, which was a standard occupant of our coffee table. Both of my parents were heavy smokers and I guess fire safety was not a huge concern yet as it was common in those years to leave lighters, in my parents' case, a big lighter, lying around.

Anyways, Lisa and I were playing with this one, and Lisa's pajamas ended up catching on fire. It was before flame-retardant material as well, and I remember her running around the living room crying and ablaze. I cannot remember how the fire was put out, but she lived through the ordeal with very little bodily damage.

Playing with fire remained in my arsenal, but a preference for matches grew. The last memory I have in this apartment was walking through the woods around the complex with a box of wooden matches. We came across an old mattress and I began lighting matches and tossing them on the mattress. I can still see clearly the matches hitting the dry fabric and the fire smoldering. We continued through the woods, but when we made our way back to the mattress, it was engulfed. I rushed back to the complex and tried to get the water hose to extinguish it before it spread, but the tap handle was not on the spigot, so I could not turn the water on. Eventually, the fire grew out of control and firefighters had to be called in, successfully putting it out before the flames made their way to the apartments.

I do not recall how I was punished or even if I was punished, but I do know we moved soon after.

Next up was an even smaller apartment at Azalea Apartments in Virginia Beach. This was the last place, the last home we would live in together as a family.

One of the most vivid memories I have of my childhood is the day my mother left my father. The day *we* left my father.

I remember it as if it were yesterday. My mother put my older sister, my younger baby brother, and me in the backseat of our VW Bug. She got in the driver's seat and then looking back at us in her platinum wig and announced, "We're leaving your father!"

I was stunned. Even at five years old, I felt the devastation. I felt my life unraveling. I am not sure I ever recovered from that moment. In fact, I think the steps that propelled that moment in time created a cataclysmic wrinkle in my life and my mother's life.

As I look back at these two, I think to myself, how different they became. I wonder if their differences brought them together. I wonder, had they always been the way I knew them? My father was a neat person. He liked things clean. My mother was almost the opposite of him. My father was quiet, while my mother was loud. When I look back, I wonder, should they have married at all?

This event is carved into my memory. My family would never be the same.

Not Married

The four of us moved into my grandparents' home on Johnson Street in Virginia Beach, and after a brief transition, life seemed to get back to normal, or as normal as I would remember. I loved living with my grandparents, as they were always very kind and caring towards us. Their home was peaceful, loving, and quiet.

My grandfather had an Alaskan Malamute named King. My mother slept in the living room and when my grandfather would let King in the house, he would run and jump on the sofa, waking her up. My grandfather used to get a kick out of that. He also had a Macaw named Sparkle. He got the bird as a baby in Panama and brought it back to the states. He could sit and have a whole conversation with that bird.

It seemed to be a good place for my mother to get her bearings, as well, because after being a homemaker for many years, she quickly rejoined the workforce. Running a household must have taught her some good leadership qualities because she held a variety of managerial positions: She was a manager of Shoney's Big Boy, a manager at Pier One and then an assistant manager of Murphy's Mart.

My grandfather's work ethic rubbed off on her, and she was finally able to break through enough for us to move out of my grandparents' house and into the newly built Palms Apartments. I would have to say this part of my life was the happiest I ever was as a child, in terms of security. Our apartment was spacious, and I do not remember ever feeling hungry, which would be a common state in the years to come. My mother was happy for the most part. She dated a few people, mostly sailors, and I remember all of them treated us with kindness.

Eventually, she began dating a man, Mark, who she became quite serious about. We even moved to Washington, DC, briefly to live with him. He was nice enough when my mother and he were just dating, but once we moved in with him his truer side began to emerge. He was very controlling; he even put a lock on the refrigerator, which did not seem to bother my mother.

It was very confusing. When there were no men in my mom's life, we were the center of her universe. She worked for us; she took care of us. She even was known to treat us like everyone else's mother. Life seemed normal. I remember one Christmas I got an Evel Knievel wind-up motorcycle. I played with it for hours; I loved it so much. My mother knew I would and just beamed with happiness watching me cruise it around the living room. Up the walls, over the couch, through the Christmas tree... I know she probably had to save for it, which I think made her proud.

Nevertheless, my mom was the type of person who always needed someone; her self-worth depended on having a man in her life. Therefore, when these guys came around, we got pushed to the side a little. If one of these men enabled or participated in her addiction to alcohol, well then, nothing else mattered, especially not her kids.

Mark and my mother would leave us alone for hours while they went out partying, even though at the time my sister was eight, I was five, and my brother was only one or so.

Finally, my mother came to her senses, but not before I had my first beating. My obsession with fire had not waned and I was lighting those long matches used to light a fireplace and throwing them over the balcony into the bushes below. When Mark caught me, he whipped me with a belt. My mother moved us back to Virginia Beach shortly after that incident. I like to think that was the reason, at least.

Most of her boyfriends were nice to us, though. They would buy us ice cream cones and take us to play putt putt, things that fathers did. One guy, Buddy, would take us down to the pool in the apartment complex and would even get in the water and play with us.

I remember one time Buddy and his friends, mostly other young Navy men, went down to the Jungle Golf putt putt course at the oceanfront. They somehow managed to steal the silverback gorilla that was cemented into the ground. They evidently cut the rebar and brought it to my mother. I do not recall what she said to them, but the gorilla did not stay long in the apartment.

None of these men wanted to marry my mother, though, at least not that I heard of. Perhaps, it was because of her cooking. My mother thinks she can cook, but she cannot. To this day, I will not eat tuna casserole; I will hardly eat tuna for that matter. She would just throw together egg noodles, cream of mushroom soup and a can of tuna and feed it to us. I hate even the thought of it. She also cooks spaghetti and the sauce in one pot. I think at one time she could cook, but laziness overtook her domestic skills, and the food became awful.

My father was scarce during this time, which only added to the confusion.

After a while, we eventually did start having visits with him, but it was usually awkward. He would pick my sister and me up, but I do not remember him ever bringing my little brother. I think this was because Ralph Jr. was still very young and my father could not take care of him.

My father had gone back to school to become a psychologist and was living in a garage, which was converted into an apartment. He had a walk-in closet where the outside wall was the garage door, which was still hooked to the electric opener. During one of my visits, I remember hitting the button and the garage door opening exposing his closet to the outside world. It was during a winter storm and my father's clothes were covered in snow.

Although my father was working to get his professional life back on track, he was still drinking. Our visits mostly consisted of us going to Charlie's Bar down on Hampton Blvd, which was walking distance from his place. He would buy us each a Shirley Temple and some sort of pub fare to eat while he drank and chatted up his bar friends. We would end up being there so late that Lisa and I would often curl up in the round booths and fall asleep.

My mom also took us to visit my grandparents a lot. The older I would get, the more I would especially love seeing my grandfather. Not only because he was really the only positive male influence in my life, but also because he was just so cool. He was my hero.

While this was the happiest I ever was as a child, my life was about to take a dark turn. I do not remember how long we lived in this apartment on our own, but I think my mother needed someone, and she chose a familiar face—Uncle John.

Uncle John

I was attending kindergarten at King's Grant Elementary in Virginia Beach when two family friends came to visit us from Austin, Texas. Uncle John and Uncle Danny were longtime friends of both my parents, so I do not remember feeling uneasy about their visit. In fact, they were always quite nice to us. But I was definitely surprised, not to mention confused when my mother announced we would be moving to Austin with Uncle John, who lived with Uncle Danny. I was sad, too, as I did not know where the hell Austin, Texas, was. It seemed a lifetime away from my grandparents, away from my dad.

I remember my last night at King's Grant, although I have no memory of my teacher or any classmates. I do remember walking back and forth to my grandparents' house and watching the Mickey Mouse Club on their television when I got there. It was mid-way during the year and there was some kind of festival. I remember I wanted to participate in the cakewalk. I am not sure why I wanted to walk around and around until the music stopped, but I won a coconut cake.

Days later, we arrived in Austin to find an apartment with no room for three kids. I recall it was on the water—a river, I think. I remember sleeping on the floor with my sister and brother, and it was the first time I felt my mother separating from my siblings and me, even more than with Mark, or Buddy or any of the other men. This move would mark the pivotal moment in time when my mother abandoned the family values and ideologies of her parents. This is the point in her own life that alcohol became more important than anything did, and it would never be the same again for her.

It was not long before arriving in Austin that I knew my

life would be different, though. By the time, we had arrived in Austin I am guessing we moved eight to ten times, and I was not even seven years old. Perhaps my mother thought Uncle John could provide some stability. However, just when our lives might have begun to come together, they would slowly and painfully unravel.

My mother and John drank all the time. Partying would become a priority over taking care of us, and even making a respectable living for that matter. Our life had not been easy up to this point, mind you, but at least we had space—and electricity.

We did not stay in that cramped apartment very long, quickly moving from place to place. I was young and do not remember the order in which we lived at each residence, however, I do vividly remember one place that was on Pin Oak Drive.

It was a decrepit blue two-story house. John and my mother slept on a mattress; my siblings and I slept on pieces of carpet. The only other furniture in the entire house was a round white table and four lawn chairs. I remember lying on my piece of carpet wondering how we could go from a nice 'home' in Virginia to this dump in such a short span of time.

I missed our apartment.

I missed my school.

I missed my grandparents' house.

I missed my dad's garage suite.

I even missed the booth at Charlie's Bar.

I remember wondering how things could possibly get worse, but they did.

In fact, the story of my life did not just take a dark turn in this two-story dump; it took an evil twist. Some of the following facts I found out later but experienced first. You see, John was gay. Uncle Danny had apparently been his partner for a long time, but as children, we did not know. My mother knew, though. In fact, Uncle Danny still lived with Uncle John, and us when we first moved to Austin. Yet on May 4, 1976, my mother married him. To this day, I do not understand why—or on the other hand, why he married her, for that matter.

This next part of my life I have shielded from my present. I have always been ashamed like it was something I had done. I have been angry for many years. I have been angry with my mother, as she knew what was happening. I have been angry with John Kilgore for stealing my youth, my childhood and for making me live in the shadows. In addition, at 48 years old I am still angry.

John molested me. And continued for years.

My mother's new husband came into my room, lied down on the floor next to me and began fondling me. I was shocked and confused, not understanding what was going on. I was too young to do anything. I felt helpless and terrified.

"I'm just trying to make you feel good," he would whisper.

Night after night, this continued. Sometimes he would masturbate while he fondled me, and sometimes he would just make me watch. I was so embarrassed that I did not tell my mother. I did not tell my siblings. I did not tell my best friend. I did not tell my teacher. I did not tell anyone.

I did not know how to react when it was happening but did everything I could to try to protect myself. As soon as my mother would turn my lights off, I would tuck my blankets under me so John could not reach in and touch me after everyone had gone to bed. I tried to spend every weekend I could away from my house, begging to stay at a friend's house. Eventually, I would even barricade my door with my dresser, but my mother said it was a fire hazard and forced me to stop.

At one point, John did get a job at a local mill reloading the vending machines. He convinced my mother that teaching me the value of hard work at a young age would be good for me, so he would take me with him at night to help him. The real reason, of course, was so he could molest me.

John also had gay friends who would come to town to visit. Some of them would try the same thing John was doing. One of these friends, "Uncle" Doug, had been around quite a long time and would try to touch me from time to time, but nothing like John. It is amazing how sexual abuse can become so relative so quickly. Uncle Doug did always try to take a picture of me as I was getting out of the shower, though. He would surprise me by standing there holding a camera. I am not sure he ever got a nude picture, and even though he would ask repeatedly, I never knowingly allowed my picture to be taken without clothes on.

It was hell. I could not protect myself, and every day I wondered how I would survive. Living in Texas was different in so many ways. My mother had started drinking heavily, and there was a total disregard for how we were treated. I cannot imagine my mother not knowing what John was doing, but in retrospect, I cannot believe how we were treated overall. We were often left by ourselves for entire evenings so they could go out drinking, with my sister, who was now about nine, put in charge of my brother who was about three and myself at the ripe old age of seven.

Who am I?

Time went on. We continued moving into different houses; John continued molesting me. I remember one of the places was on Flournoy Ave. This house was even more deplorable than the two-story if that is even possible. The floor in one of the rooms was actually caving in. We had to keep the door closed so that my little brother would not toddle in and fall through. We were literally living hand to mouth, barely having enough for our basic needs.

I am not sure how long we lived there, but I remember that this was where I was told I would no longer be a Sroufe. That is right, out of the blue one day, I came home from school and my mother informed me that she had changed my and my siblings' last name to Kilgore.

"You, you mean he's my... father now?" I could barely get the words out.

My mother smiled awkwardly. "Well, no not officially. But your real father is a son-of-a-bitch deadbeat."

She could see the tears well in my eyes, so tried to convince me this was a good thing, "John has been more like a dad to you than anyone. You should be happy and grateful to have his name."

I was neither.

John was a slimy man who preyed on me, but beyond that, there was still nothing to be proud of. He was lazy, slightly overweight and had false upper teeth that were not even complete. He was a liar and a crook who obviously did not care about paying a bill.

He yelled all the time and beat my brother and me. We were small and not used to it. I remember adults yelling and screaming, but never someone laying their hands upon us in a violent matter, other than maybe a slight smack to get out attention. Nothing like this— ever. Even when my mother's boyfriend Mark beat me for starting the fire, it was nothing like what my brother and I began to experience at the hands of John.

In addition, here my mother was telling me that I would now share the same last name as this monster. She slid the telephone over to me and dialed. "I think it's best your dad hears it from you. It will make him feel better if he knows you're happy about it."

My dad answered and with my mother watching me, I broke the news to him. It had been one of the first times we had spoken since my mother had taken us away from him to live in Austin, and I could hear the heartbreak his voice.

His voice quivered. "Of course, Bill. I'm okay with it if you're okay with it."

Therefore, just like that, I became someone different, no official paperwork, nothing. I was enrolled in school as Bill Kilgore. Now, not only did I hate my home, I hated my name. I have report cards, certificates, etc. that say 'Bill Kilgore' on them and to this day, it has taken all of my willpower not to rip them up.

Third-grade Breakdown

The last year we lived in Austin, John was in prison. The odd thing is I do not recall him being arrested or some cataclysmic event leading up to him being in jail. I do not remember a trial or anything. I just remember going to visit him.

He had been convicted of robbery for, I think, stealing the bank bags from where he was working. Although you would think him being put away would be some sort of respite, this was equally a tumultuous time in my childhood. By this point, we had moved more times than I could count, and we were continuing to live in places with no heat or furniture. Of course, I was grateful that John could not touch me on a daily or nightly basis, but as I would come to understand years later, victims of abuse do not always deal with things in a rational, predictable way.

Especially not in third grade. It was traumatic for a kid. Moreover, for people who are abused, you take on this different role. You always think you are doing something wrong. Guilt, shame, and anxiety become your go-to emotion, even when you are not even directly involved.

I was attending Brentwood Elementary at the time and my teacher was Ms. Zimmerman. I remember her in typical 70s fashion with big hair, and big glasses. I was quite fond of her, probably because she was so kind and caring towards me. I never told her what was going on in my home life, though. She must have thought something was wrong with me as I was always stressed out about a number of things, like not having enough food and having to go visit the man who molested me in jail on the weekends—not anything I should have ever had to deal with at eight years old.

All these years later, it is fascinating to me when I tell my story to people who have known me for years. They are surprised to find out I came from such poverty. Many colleagues have even told me they assumed I grew up wealthy, and that I went into education for a hobby or some greater good. Now I am quite reserved and very structured, but when I was a child, I was an emotional wreck. Mrs. Zimmerman can attest to that.

One day, I guess the stress became too much and I broke down in her classroom. It was more than a breakdown; I burst into a full-fledged panic attack. Mrs. Zimmerman tried to calm me down, but I was inconsolable. I was hysterical, apparently because John was in jail. She called my mother and it was one of the only times I remember her coming into my school.

I can see her in my mind's eye walking down the hallway as I stood outside my third-grade classroom shaking.

"That's her," I said to Mrs. Zimmerman.

Mrs. Zimmerman and my mother then went inside the classroom without me to talk. If this would have happened today, child psychologists would have been called in and I probably would have been put on medication. Nevertheless, this was the 70s, so my mother just took me home. Soon, I would finish the third grade in another state.

I did have a few good memories in Texas, though. I remember the pencil machine on the wall at Odom Elementary, the first school I went to. I was fascinated that I could put in a nickel and a pencil would come out. I never had a nickel, mind you, but I always wanted to buy a pencil from that machine. I also remember going to Lake Travis to swim. We would sit there and watch the hummingbirds. They were everywhere. There was also a great barbeque restaurant we would go to. It is funny what the mind remembers.

Ellenboro

Halfway through the third grade, John was released from prison and we moved to Ellenboro, North Carolina, because that is where my grandparents were now living. This was the hometown of my grandfather. The five of us moved into my great grandparents' house, but my great grandmother, Adeline, died soon after our arrival. It was still a houseful as there were the five of us there along with my great grandfather, grandfather, and grandmother. My great grandfather built the house. It was a quaint home, with paneled rooms and carpet. The kitchen was efficient; it had a breakfast bar where I could sit and talk to my grandfather while he worked in the kitchen. There was always something to drink at their house, and always a snack.

In the living room, there was a round coffee table with a blue and green plaid couch. They always had hard candy and nuts on the end tables and we were always able to have however much we wanted. My grandmother and grandfather had their own chair on separate sides of the living room. It had a smell of clean. I am not sure how to describe it beyond that, but it made me feel comfortable.

The bathroom smelled of Ivory soap and there were powders, perfumes, and colognes everywhere. There were three bedrooms. My grandparents slept in the front bedroom, and then there were two bedrooms at the back of the house. I only saw inside one of the bedrooms at the back once, as my grandmother used it as a closet.

It made me so happy to be living with my grandparents again. Not only because we had food, heat, and electricity, but also because I knew John would not dare touch me at their house. Not under the same roof as my grandfather. My hero, my namesake—William E. Greene—was truly a man above men and John was scum under his boot. My grandfather was a WWII Navy veteran; a Pearl Harbor survivor. John was a criminal.

Every time I was with him, my grandfather would tell me stories of his adventures while he was in the military. He would tell me about the attack on Pearl Harbor and how he was woken up by screaming sailors yelling, "Wake up! Wake up! We're being attacked!"

He would tell me stories of taking Admiral Block's boat out into the harbor to find survivors, and how they had to leave the dead bodies, many of his friends, behind. After the attack, he said he stayed up for 36 hours straight and when he returned he just threw his clothes away, got two sandwiches and a fifth of bourbon, and slept for about four hours. Then he went right back out.

My grandfather was a hard worker and an old school provider. In fact, my grandmother never worked a day in her life, even though at times my grandfather had to work two jobs. He retired from the Navy in 1965 and went to work for the Balboa Company as an engineer on the Panama Canal. He always had a side business or was taking a class to learn something new.

I often wonder how my mother could have been raised by this fascinating, honorable man, but marry someone like John. I often wonder how my grandfather tolerated her daughter marrying such a low-life.

My father always spoke highly of my grandfather; he respected him, and my grandfather had the same respect for my father. The same was not true for John. I am sure my grandfather did not have a clue that I had been molested, and I was too afraid to tell anyone, much less him. In fact, if he were alive I could have never written this book. It would have broken his heart if he had known.

He knew how we had been living, though. He could see how my mother had changed. She had one sister, and my grandmother had lost a baby boy, but she was clearly my grandfather's favorite. They were very much alike, and my mother had grown distant over the years, only coming around to borrow money or ask for favors. The alcohol had changed who she was in many ways, including her relationship with her father. I would say that it even affects her to this day.

Shortly after we arrived, I started Ellenboro Elementary. Coming from Austin, Texas, where I was an unclean little boy who blended into the background, Ellenboro Elementary was a breath of fresh air.

My teacher was Miss King. She had short hair and was kind and very conscientious. I learned my multiplication tables in her class, but that, of course, is not what made her class so lovely. I got my first two girlfriends, that year - Susan Humphries and Tammy Hawkins. Not at the same time, of course.

It was also that year that I met my best friend, Scott Hoppes, although our first meeting was not so lovely. I had to walk across the railroad tracks to catch the school bus and I do not remember why, but on this day, I was arguing with another kid. Not that arguing with other boys was unusual. Perhaps it was pent-up anger, always needing to be on the defense or feeling like a pathetic wimp at home, but I often felt like I needed to act like a tough guy out in the "real world," even at such a young age.

I told this kid I was going to slug him, and Scott, who was his friend, came up to me and said, "You want to fight? Fight me instead."

Scott was a slender kid, not terribly tall, but not short either, with a thinner face and thick hair. I remember his sister describing him once as looking like a German Shepherd. He was stoic, even at such a young age, and I backed down.

We shook hands and Scott said we should be friends. I agreed. Imagine if all conflicts could be settled so easily.

Scott was a Dallas Cowboys fan and so was I, so that was the decisive factor. We were friends for life. I spent so much time at his house, I am sure his parents got tired of me.

We would hike through the woods and build dams in the creek—normal boyhood stuff. That is what it was: being friends with Scott made me feel like a regular kid. His family, as you will see, would become so important to how my life unfolded I cannot even describe it.

In the spring, we moved into a house down from my grandparents and my nightmare life soon took up where it had left off in Austin. My bedroom did not have any windows and at one time was used to cure meat. Living in that bedroom was an awkward experience at best. It was always dark; it is hard to believe that a third grader would have to live in a room without windows. It may have been fitting for that time in my life, though, as there was no escape and nowhere to look to escape. It seems very symbolic looking back.

John began molesting me again and soon started in on my brother, who was now, I guess, "of age" in his books. It is hard to describe the chaos of being molested and someone who is supposed to be taking care of you doing something so horrible. Eventually, he began molesting other boys as well; or at least, I began witnessing it. There was one time John was going off to haul trash and needed help so told me I had to come along. My friend Robert was over, so I felt relieved that John would not be able to do anything if Robert came with us. Surely, he would not touch me in front of another kid. However, when we got to the dump, John left me in the car. Robert obviously did not know about John, because he eagerly jumped out of the truck to help. I watched, paralyzed with fear and shame as John took Robert behind a tree and pulled Robert's pants down.

Robert and I never talked about that. But another time, my friend Eddie told me John asked if he could touch him. On the outside, I just blew it off as if he was joking, but inside I was frightened and mortified.

Eddie never came back to my house again.

Johns' "friends" would again come to visit from time to time, and again ask to take pictures of me when I got out of the bath. No one else touched me, but I was always on guard.

With friends dwindling, I would try to stay at my grandparents' house as often as possible. I still never told them what was going on, but I am sure they were not happy with what their daughter's life had become, and could understand why I did not want to be at home.

Nearing the end of my third-grade year, my mother had my half-sister Leigh Anne on April 8, 1979. I do not recall my mother's pregnancy. We were crowded into that small house, and while I do not recall her drinking or smoking during the pregnancy, she certainly picked it back up when Leigh Anne was born.

By the end of the third grade, we had moved into a new trailer. The trailer sat on property that once belonged to my great grandmother. My brother and I shared the front room. We had bunk beads. I always slept on top. Our new home did not remain "new" very long. It quickly became a den of debauchery and filth. The older I got, the further I wanted to be away. There was always a smell of stale alcohol and cigarette smoke. I look back now and it was almost as if we were homeless people living temporarily in this place. We lived hand-to-mouth, and I always wondered where the next meal came from as I watched my mother and John eek every minute they were living into an alcoholic stupor. There was no time for cleaning or gathering up clutter. I did not live in a home, but a lair poised for malcontent, clutter, and filth. I escaped when I could, but it was never enough.

It is hard to believe I was coming of age at the end of the third grade. I began to take note of the government cheese and powdered milk. My mother would not make the milk in advance and would not allow us to measure it. We often had warm watery milk, and a small cheese sandwich.

The new place quickly gave John an opportunity to continue to molest me, as our bedroom was at the front of the trailer, and they added a building on as their room. I quickly learned to stay away as much as I could, but the dark of the night gave him the opportunity he needed.

Fourth Grade

My fourth grade was the year I met some of the people I still consider my closest friends. Our teacher was Mrs. Butler. Like Miss King, she was kind and a good teacher. She was very attentive, but there was no nonsense in her class. The rock group KISS was popular at the time, and a couple of my friends and I wanted to form a KISS Club. Mrs. Butler was not having it. Even after we made KISS identification cards for everyone, she shut us down paralleling the group with Satan and young boys being lost before they really got going. We did what was told and detached ourselves, at least while she was looking, from the rock group.

I do not remember this, but some 30 years later Michael Blanton, one of my friends, reminded me that when she said no, we formed a club named the "Sparklers" instead. I am sure KISS would have been impressed.

None of us could sing, of course, so perhaps that is why I chose to forget. John continued to molest me; he began preying on my friends, and my younger brother. Sometimes I wonder how many young boys he affected. Maybe that is why I cannot remember sometimes, because maybe I chose not to remember.

Peeping Holes and Glass Doors

The last place I lived in Ellenboro was a trailer that was purchased my fourth-grade year. The structure of it changed many times as John and my mother attempted to "add on". My bedroom was in a constant state of upheaval as well, but sadly, by this time I was used to it. It was right across from my mother and John's room. I think it was really supposed to be a storage room, as it was only wide enough for a bed and a dresser and again did not have windows.

For a time, there was only one bathroom that, for a while, was also home to the washing machine. There was an inset in the wall with the connections to the drain, as well as the hot and cold water. The room on the other side of the bathroom was my sister's bedroom and John drilled a hole in the inset, where there was only a piece of paneling. When my brother or I would go to the bathroom or take a shower, he would go into Lisa's room and watch us.

Whenever we had friends over, he would do the same to them.

When I finally realized what was going on, I would put my clothes up to block the "peephole." John would get very angry, but I had started to become defiant, so would keep doing it. Eventually, he got so irate he whipped me with a belt, and he did not stop peeping either. If I had a friend over, John would encourage us to use the bathroom together or take a bath, so, of course, he could go in Lisa's room to watch us. One time, a friend of mine was using the bathroom and noticed an eye in the peephole. Thinking it was my little brother he poked it. Realizing it was John, he said he was going to tell his father, but John insisted it was Ralph. I do not remember anything else happening after that incident when I had friends over. Of course, at that point, I rarely had friends over, for that reason.

Aside from my fear of John touching one of my friends, I also was embarrassed by my surroundings. What should have been a joyful time in my life was not as it was marred by these events; it was side-railed by managing something a child should not have to manage. The endless ashtrays and filth embarrassed me. There was always that smell of staleness.

By this time, any resemblance of a normal life was long gone. We were living in a filthy trailer, mangled together with two other trailers, attempting, I guess, to look like a house. It was a horrendous sight. The front porch cover was pieced together with scrap wood and when the board was not long enough, John would just nail boards together.

Our electricity would occasionally be turned off because of lack of payment, and I remember John going to the box, cutting off the lock and turning the power back on. He put more effort into trying to cut corners and get freebies than he did trying to make a living. There is an emptiness as a child when the people who are supposed to provide for you do not seem to care anything about you.

Even with simple misunderstandings, there was chaos. There was an incident on one Mother's Day when we kids had bought my mother a new robe. I was excited for her, as new things were not readily something that came into our house and presents were certainly a scarcity. The robe we got her was similar, if not the same as the one she already had, but obviously new. It was long, cream in color and fuzzy, a winter-style robe.

It was a warm Sunday morning, and so I had been outside playing. I was just walking into the trailer through the side glass door when John stumbled out of the bedroom half-asleep and fully hungover.

My mother was sitting in her recliner drinking coffee in what I thought was her new robe.

Upset, I asked, "Did they give you your present without me?"

Without giving her a chance to answer or me to explain what had happened, John's eyes widened with rage, and he hit me so hard that I went through the glass door and off the porch of the trailer.

Mayhem ensued. My mother had not even heard my question, so did not know why John had hit me. John seemed most upset about the shattered glass door.

I took off—cut, battered and crying. I ran around to the back of the trailer screaming in pain. John and my mother came looking for me. I tried to hide, but I could not stop crying. I was cowering on the side of the house near the back porch when they found me. I was truly terrified.

My mother was crying and apologizing. John kept repeating that he was sorry and tried to get me to come back inside with him. I refused. Eventually, they got me back to where they put ice on my back and nursed the cuts with iodine.

Between the tears, I tried to explain that I thought John had given her the Mother's Day present without me, when in reality she had her old robe on. John was upset thinking I had ruined the surprise of the new robe, thus his angry reaction, which I guess he thought was reasonable. I do not remember giving her the actual new robe, and after picking up the glass, everyone went about their "normal" way of life.

Fifth Grade

In the fifth grade, I had a wonderful teacher named Miss Williamson. She was the only African-American teacher at the school that I recall, and for sure was the only one I ever had. She was incredibly caring not only to me but to the whole class. In retrospect, I realize she must have known something was wrong with my home life. I was dirty and unkempt, yet I came to school every single day. As any teacher or administrator can tell you, it is not uncommon for children who are growing up in poverty or who are not taken care of physically, to miss a lot of school, especially during that era. Education and attendance were just not always a priority for children who had other barriers, but it was for me.

Not especially because I loved to learn. I just hated being at home with two unemployed alcoholics.

Miss Williamson was really a kind soul. She would give me odd jobs to do in the classroom and pay me a quarter so I could buy ice cream. She would even buy me a snack or a cola after school herself.

Although a wonderful teacher, Miss Williamson would sometimes fall asleep in class. All the students liked her, but we were kids, so had a mischievous side. After she would assign us seatwork, we would all be extremely quiet to see if she would fall asleep.

Slowly, but surely, her eyes would close.

One time while she was falling asleep, she must have caught herself because she jerked her head quickly, and her front teeth flew across the classroom. That is right; Miss Williamson also had false teeth that apparently were not secured properly. It took all of my strength not to burst out laughing, and I am sure the rest of the class felt the same, but you could have heard a pin drop in this room full of usually rambunctious fifth graders as Miss Williamson walked over, picked her teeth off the ground and put them back in her mouth.

Hope out of pain

It is hard for me to know who my mother was before she became an alcoholic. I remember at times she had been a hard worker, which she got from her father, and as I mentioned earlier, when there were no men in her life, her children were her world. However, men were not her only vice—alcohol was equally destructive. Once drinking took over her life, she became mean. She seemed to like to yell a lot. She was always yelling. I remember being a kid and wondering how someone could yell so much. She also became uncaring of what happened to her children.

Her drink of preference was a screwdriver. I am not sure if she thought the orange juice somehow made drinking them incessantly healthy, but she would get killer hangovers. Every morning after the night before, she would send me to Thomas Tisdale, the greengrocery in Ellenboro, to get her a Mountain Dew or across the street to the Pepsi machine at Jack Green's garage.

It is a small town, Mr. Tisdale would grant people credit and even cash checks. With neither John nor my mother working on a regular basis, we always had a tab. When I was in the 5th grade, around mid-December, I remember receiving a card in the mail from my father for my birthday and it had five dollars in it. There were not many places to spend five dollars in Ellenboro, so I went to Tisdale to buy some candy. Mr. Tisdale just frowned, informing me that he could not sell me anything because my mother and her husband had not paid their account in months. I asked how much they owed and he told me they owed close to $35 dollars.

I gave Mr. Tisdale my $5 bill. I was proud of myself at first because I was able to help, then angry because I had to use my birthday money to pay their bill and never got any candy. I walked home defeated.

Ellenboro was a typical small town in many ways, especially when it came to gossip. There was not much that someone did not know about someone else.

Given my mother and John's very gossip-worthy lifestyle, it was no surprise that they had to go beyond town limits to find people who wanted to hang out with them, eventually, striking up a friendship with Bob, a guy who lived across the county in Rutherfordton. Bob was a soft-spoken overweight man, with stringy hair, bad teeth, and a beard. He was from up North—Michigan I think—so I always thought he spoke very odd.

When they first started hanging out with Bob, we would go with them to his house but were just put in a back room. Bob had cable television at his house, and it was the first time I ever saw HBO. We still had an antenna on our trailer and only received four or five channels. The television kept us kids busy while they got drunk.

One time, actually the only time I ever saw my mother smoke marijuana, was in Rutherfordton. It was winter and my mother and I were with Bob's brother Cary out running errands (i.e. picking up booze and munchies). Cary was driving, my mother was in the passenger seat and I was crammed in the backseat of the two-door beater.

When we got to the grocery store, Cary parked. I thought we were getting out, but then Cary proceeded to roll a joint. I thought it was just a regular cigarette but once he lit it, the smell was so awful I kept asking what it was.

Cary scoffed, "Pot, kid. Wanna try?" Then he burst out laughing as he took a drag. My mother just stared at me but took the joint when Cary offered it to her.

She and Cary passed it back and forth a few times, as I sat anxiously in the backseat.

"Pot?" I thought to myself. I remembered hearing about some teenagers who had been expelled from the high school in Ellenboro when they got caught smoking pot in the parking lot. The principal of my school came around from class to class and explained that marijuana was illegal and those kids could have been put in jail.

As Cary and my mother smoked up, I was checking the parking lot, wondering if the cops might come get us too.

Because it was quite cold out, the windows were rolled up, so in addition to my worries of being busted, I was also getting high from the secondhand smoke. I started to panic—crying, begging to get out of the car. As I was in the back of a two-door, I was trapped, which only intensified my anxiety.

Finally, I started to scream, and my mother relented, opening her door. I squeezed myself out and breathed in the icy cold air. I started to cough and gag, sitting on the curb while they finished their joint.

Eventually, Cary got out and entered the grocery store. My mother's door flung open and she jumped out, furious. She smacked me across the face and said, "Get back in the goddamn car and stop being such a baby!"

Apparently, smoking pot was not as relaxing for my mother as it is for some.

She stormed into the store. I opened both car doors and waited for them there, eyes peeled for cops, while the car aired out.

It wasn't too long after that event that my siblings and I no longer went to Rutherfordton with them, and even though Rutherfordton is about 15 miles away from Ellenboro, they would leave us home alone in that trailer. My older sister was about twelve and I was ten, so together we would take care of my brother who was six and my younger sister who was just a toddler. Often they would leave early in the day and not come back until after we were asleep.

It was on one of these nights away, that I thought for sure they would finally stop drinking. After all, they say nothing can change the trajectory of one's life like a tragedy.

It was the winter of 1980, when after a long day and night of partying, John and Bob, both extremely drunk, left to get more alcohol from the grocery store in Rutherfordton. Bob was driving and on the way, he hit another car.

They killed an entire family.

Both men had life-threatening injuries, as well, with John sustaining a head injury that required more than a hundred stitches.

Before I knew what had occurred, I remember being at home alone with my siblings in the trailer all day. It was cold out and so had been pent up inside. We went to bed early, but at about 3 AM, I got up. I quickly realized they were not home yet but began combing the trailer for them anyway. I even checked the deck for footprints and the driveway for tire tracks, but to no avail.

I called Bob's house; no one answered. By now, I was frantic!

Suddenly, the phone rang. It was my mother, crying hysterically. She explained what had happened and said they would be home soon.

I could not go back to sleep, so I just continued to lie there, thinking, *THIS will make them stop drinking. This has got to.*

Looking back, I realize kids should not have to think about things like that.

Bob ended up in jail for vehicular homicide; my mother and John never stopped drinking.

Bartender and Orange Juice

I am not sure when I learned that most people drank orange juice for breakfast; I always thought it was meant as a mixer for a screwdriver. We had orange juice in the house, but it was off limits to my siblings and me. And even though the directions read three parts water to one part concentrate, I had to mix one part concentrate to whatever the container would hold in water. It barely resembled orange juice but paired well with cheap vodka. Before I was in middle school, I mixed more 7&7s and screwdrivers than most bartenders do in a New York City bar in six months.

I took on the role of the savior and tried to regulate my mother's intake. I would make the drink and then pour the alcohol last in hopes she would taste it and think it was strong enough and maybe stop drinking for the night. It never seemed to work, but I always tried.

The truth about growing up in this environment is that I was never shielded from alcohol. I was never shielded from the ugliness of being drunk or the abuse that is often intertwined in the bottle. In fact, I often thought I was right in the center of the madness. You feel like the world is falling down upon you and, of course, some take desperate measures. I would often escape with my friends, and later into my writing.

Clothesline

Not only did the drinking continue, so did the molesting.

The trailer we were living in was situated on a three-acre plot of land that was once my great grandmother's flower garden. It was mostly wide-open field with the exception of a small pine tree forest at the back of the property behind our trailer.

My summers were spent outside wandering around exploring the unknown, hanging out with my friends and trying to make new ones. The more friends I had, the more places I could go for sleepovers. I had become an expert at finding ways to stay away from home, especially at night to avoid John coming into my room while my mother was passed out.

It is really an awful thing when a child does not feel safe in his or her own bedroom. When darkness equals violation.

However, that is what my life was, night after night. Therefore, in the summertime, when I could not find a friend's house to sleep at, I would camp outside. I did not have a real tent, of course, so I would build a fort in the pine tree forest using the wooden picnic table and benches.

In Ellenboro, we were related to many people, mostly cousins. One day, I was down at my cousins' trailer visiting, and they asked me to stay the night. I told them I was going to sleep outside and they asked me where. I explained to them where in the woods I had set up camp.

A few hours later, we all went home. It was nighttime by now, so I retreated to my "campsite" without my mother or anyone noticing. I was almost asleep when I heard a branch break. Then another and then another. John.

Stumbling drunk. Unbeknownst to me, John must have been nearby listening when I was telling my cousins what I was up to; or perhaps he had gone to my bedroom for a "visit" and discovered I was gone.

Still, in the distance, I could hear him traipsing through the trees. My stomach churned. I knew if I stayed there, he would have me trapped under the picnic table, so I eased my way out in the darkness, to try to make my way back to the trailer without him seeing me. No luck.

"Bill!" he yelled. I began to run.

This infuriated him, so he started chasing me. Nothing made John angrier than having to chase his prey. Knowing what would happen if I stopped, I ran harder. Even though it was dark and I could not see anything except for one light on in the trailer, I raced as fast as I could. I was almost on the porch when I ran into the crosswire that tethered down the clothesline post. I hit it so hard with my chest that I actually did a flip around the wire. I was not wearing a shirt and the rusty wire penetrated my skin, leaving a welt from my ear to pelvis.

I began to cry, agonizing in pain.

John finally caught up and out of breath, scolded, "It serves you right for running away!"

By this point, I was screaming, but my mother still never came out of the trailer. I assumed she was passed out. John slinked inside. Not knowing what would happen, a touching or a beating if I went to my bedroom, I thought my best option was to go to get as far away as I could from John. I went back to my campsite and tried to keep watch, but ended up crying myself to sleep.

The next morning, I went to my grandparents' house, which was on the other side of the field near the dirt road. As my grandfather gently applied Mercurochrome on my wound, he asked me what had happened, but I was too frightened to explain. I told them it was an accident.

It seems I would have many "accidents" when I was young.

Mrs. Frances Bailey

Having been an educator now for nearly 20 years, I am humbled by the students I encounter and the extraordinary work I see happening to benefit kids. Miss Williamson was a great fifth-grade teacher who showed me that humanity was alive and well, but what I owe to this world, who I owe to what I have and who I have become, is Mrs. Frances Bailey.

Mrs. Bailey was my sixth-grade math teacher. A teacher who knew kids, who knew how to build a relationship with a troubled, abused, dirty, loud-mouthed little boy who was in desperate need of a haircut. The year I had Mrs. Bailey was a troubled one, yet I still never missed a day of school. The abuse I suffered at home had escalated, and I was too small to fight back. I never told anyone at school, in fact before this book, I have told very few people just how bad the abuse—physical, emotional and sexual—had gotten.

Mrs. Bailey somehow knew, though, or I felt like she knew, that something awful was going on with me. She may not have known the details, but she knew I was troubled. She would look at me with so much compassion. However, her response was not to just placate or feel sorry for me; no, Mrs. Bailey helped. She extended the job description of a teacher well into that of a caregiver.

Although I had not been able to see the chalkboard for years, it was not until the sixth grade that I got my first set of glasses. The only reason I got them was that Mrs. Bailey somehow arranged for me to go to an optometrist. Usually getting glasses is not the highlight for a boy in the sixth grade, but I loved mine. When I look at my school picture from that year it makes me smile—because I am smiling in the picture. Mrs. Bailey helped me smile a lot that year. She knew me being able to see what I was doing was vital to my academic success, but she also arranged for me to go to a dentist that year as well. In fact, I would not see a dentist again for more than three years.

Even though Mrs. Bailey obviously took her vow of *in loco parentis* well beyond the call of duty, it was her ability to connect on a real level that made her so special. One of the most important conversations I remember having with Mrs. Bailey was right outside her classroom door. I remember it so clearly. This simple conversation would actually turn out to be one of the most pivotal conversations I would have in my life.

I was having an especially troubling day and was talking too much in class. Mrs. Bailey asked me to go outside of the classroom and wait for her.

I am not sure why, but as I stood outside that door I was even more anxious than usual. It was not uncommon for me to be kicked out of class, but I had grown really fond of Mrs. Bailey and did not like to disappoint her. I waited out there for a long time thinking about my behavior and thinking about my home life. Finally, she came out and asked me what was going on. I do not remember the entire conversation, though I can still see her standing in front of me in my mind's eye.

She was bent down toward me listening intently as I shared with her my emotional struggles. How at eleven years old, I was trying to carve out a person in a life I did not want to be in. How I constantly felt weak and hopeless.

Mrs. Bailey simply puts her hand on my shoulder and said, "Bill, you are going to have to have some courage. You can do anything with courage."

For the first time in my whole life, I felt relief.

Looking back now, it is amazing how one person's words

can just affect you so deeply. I thought the world of Mrs. Bailey and trusted she would not lie to me. I looked back at her and thought to myself, *Wow, if Mrs. Bailey says I can do it… then maybe I can.*

Now, I had no idea how I could get this courage, or when it would come, but still, something changed that day. I knew right then that my life would be different. Somehow, Mrs. Bailey had convinced me that I could do anything I wanted so long as I had the courage to do it. Suddenly, there was hope. I believed her, and although there was no grand epiphany or realization of how and what I could accomplish, I felt secure in the world.

Having Mrs. Bailey for sixth grade was not the end of her influence in my life. I took what she said to me, what she did for me, and carried it with me. Do not get me wrong; I would love to say that every decision I have made was based upon her words of encouragement or what she taught me, but often those lessons are lost on us for years.

Later that fall, I did have the first opportunity to utilize my newfound courage, though, when Ellenboro Elementary announced they were putting on a talent show. Most of the acts were kids tap dancing or performing baton routines, but my friend Charles and I, still huge KISS fans, decided to sing "Beth."

We practiced like crazy and went to all the rehearsals, but on the day we were to perform, Charles tried to back out. I begged him relentlessly not to desert me, trying to convince him there was no need to be afraid.

Moreover, he did not let me down. Therefore, on November 21, 1980, our two-man KISS club finally got its moment to sparkle. We took to the stage, and with Denise Martin accompanying us on the piano, serenaded the entire Ellenboro Elementary student body with the ballad to end all ballads. My childhood friends still talk about it—and not because we were good.

The sixth grade was the first year that I would have different teachers for some of the subjects. Therefore, in addition to Mrs. Bailey, I also had Mrs. Smith, who taught English, and Mr. Litaker.

Mr. Litaker taught history and PE. He was one of those teachers who would give the class an activity to do or assignment to work on and then leave, putting a student in charge to take names of anyone misbehaving.

One day, during history class, he did just that. I have no idea why, but when he returned, the pre-appointed student told him I had gotten out of my seat while he was out of the room. This was definitely a regular occurrence. It was very difficult for me to sit still in the best of times, only this time I had stayed put the entire time.

Mr. Litaker took me outside the classroom and grabbed a witness teacher on his way. I knew what this meant because teachers always had to have another one present when using physical discipline on a student.

Mr. Litaker pulled out his paddle and said, "You, Mr. Kilgore, are getting three licks."

I had no idea what was going on so asked, "Why?"

He told me what I was accused of doing, but I denied it. I had had many paddlings up to this point in my schooling and would readily admit when I had done something wrong. Okay, maybe not readily, but eventually I would own up. However, I was not going to be disciplined for something I did not do.

I stood firm in my innocence. "You are not going to paddle me," I said.

Mr. Litaker was taken back by my refusal, and probably a bit embarrassed by the lack of authority I was showing him in front of another teacher. However, with my adamant denial, he could not hit me. Frustrated, he said that my mother had to come in and speak to him. He then went back to the classroom and pulled a number of kids out. They all told him the same thing—that I had done nothing while he was out.

I do not remember my mother coming to school, but that does not mean Mr.

Litaker never called her. By then, my mother had developed a firm belief in *in loco parentis* as well, but not for the right reasons. Either way, Mr. Litaker never treated me any different. In fact, I remember him once telling me he would get me one way or the other. I am still waiting.

Ice Cream

One of the joys of attending Ellenboro Elementary was that every day nearly everyone got ice cream—those with a quarter, that is. They had all my favorites available: Nutty Buddies, ice cream sandwiches and Creamsicles, just to name a few. I had a lot of favorites, but not much disposable cash, so I used to always try to get the job of taking the orders from the students in class and then going to the ice cream room to fill the order. Most of my teachers would allow me to get an ice cream in return—most. I have searched my memory, but for the life of me, I cannot remember the teacher who would get me to take all the orders, but never allow me to get an ice cream as my reward.

I have learned that guilt and shame are the two most difficult emotions to let go of. I know this because at nearly fifty years old, I still feel remorseful that one day, after filling the order for all the other kids, I took an ice cream without paying. The principal, Mr. York, caught me and gave me three licks with his leather paddle. He also said I would have to pay off my 25 cent debt.

I remember it was a Friday, so I had all weekend to try to collect a quarter. I spent the whole weekend searching high and low for every penny I could. When I tell you that I also spent the whole weekend worried. Believe me, I was worried. It was not only the thought of another paddling that I feared; it was facing the mortification of being known as a thief. I wondered how John could have ever gotten over the humiliation of going to prison for robbery, but it never seemed to bother him. Maybe it is because he never had to pay the money back. I, however, did.

It is amazing looking back now how much a quarter meant and how scarce loose change was around our house. Finally, I was able to round up 25 cents and hid it in my room.

On Monday, I left for school early, walking the whole way. I wanted to get to Mr. York first thing with my reimbursement of what I had taken before any other students arrived. I was so ashamed; I did not want anyone to know why I was there and what I had done.

Mr. York took the money, but as I was leaving, said to me, "If you ever want an ice cream, Bill, just come see me."

This escapade happened in the seventh grade, which for some reason began a two- year span of accumulating a lot of shame around my impoverished life.

Because Ellenboro Elementary was such a small school, you would often have some of the same teachers for both the seventh and eighth grades. For example, I had the same homeroom teacher both years. Every day, while doing attendance, she would say my name: "Bill Kilgore."

"Here," I would reply.

"Do you have your lunch money?" she would ask. However, before I could answer, she would scoff, "Oh, never mind, you get free lunch."

The truth is a lot of us got free lunch, and she may not have done it every day, but she did it enough times that I still remember. Even at almost fifty years old, I remember how awful and small it made me feel. I realize she probably did not know what she was doing, at least I hope not, but in the same way, Mrs. Bailey's words lifted me up, my homeroom teacher tore me down.

Without being able to articulate it, I was truly learning to understand the power of words. At home, I would often write random words and thoughts and even short stories in a journal I had. Little did I know what this seemingly instinctual act would mean in my life.

Eighth Grade

By the time the eighth grade rolled around, I was a mess and school had become my safe-haven. In fact, I never missed a day of school my entire eighth grade year. I particularly liked reading and was quite good at it. By the end of the seventh grade, I had finished the reading series for the seventh and eighth grade. There were a few of us that had accomplished this, and I remember Mrs. Jones allowing us to be "teacher helpers" for the other grades.

We would sort papers, run copies on the mimeograph, and help tutor younger kids. One day, Michael Blanton and I were sent to make copies of some papers for one teacher; I remember one of them was a *Dukes of Hazard* coloring sheet. I drew a mustache on Daisy Duke, made copies and then handed them out to the class. For some reason, the teacher did not think it was as funny as we did. We were not invited back to help in her class.

For math, I had Mrs. Martha Freeman. She was a distant cousin, and just loved kids. She wanted all of us to be successful. Math was not my strongest subject, and it seemed like for the entire time I spent in her classroom I sat beside her checking student papers. I think she thought I would learn the material if I just kept seeing the answers repeatedly. I am still not a strong math student, though.

My first introduction to poetry occurred in Mrs. Hamrick's eighth grade English class. She would read the poems and then we had to analyze them orally and in writing. Sometimes she would get us to pick one to memorize and recite it in front of the class. I remember a few students did "Casey at the Bat" by Ernest L. Thayer, but I chose "The Highwayman" by Alfred Noyes.

The wind was a torrent of darkness among the gusty trees...

It was like nothing I had ever read. It was elegant. I was hooked.

Being exposed to poetry in Mrs. Hamrick's class made me realize that most of what I was writing in my journal at home was actually poetry. Once I labeled my work as "poems," my feelings towards them changed. I continued writing, of course, but then would smash the papers up and stuff them into a Cale Yarborough model race car box I had. I hid the box under my bed so no one would find my poems. Poetry writing was social death for a teenage boy in the early 80s.

I also had a teacher named Greg Baker who was my science teacher that year. Mr. Baker was a tall man with glasses; he reminded me of the Professor from Gilligan's Island. I used to love his classes. They were heaven for a curious boy, as he would have us do all kinds of experiments, which I thoroughly enjoyed.

Years later, when I had become a science teacher myself, I went back to Ellenboro for one of my very few visits. I went to the convenience store Mr. Baker now owned to thank him for being such a good teacher. There is nothing particular that stands out about his class except that he was a teacher that believed in building relationships. He made me feel like I was a smart kid and had value, even though I got more than one paddling from him. In those days, they gave you three licks for just about anything. I was always smarting off or not doing what I was supposed to be doing, and other teachers would have him paddle me thinking it would matter (or hurt) more from him, I guess. Still, I always thought Mr. Baker was fair.

It is funny when you go back to see someone after years of being away. I was a grown adult, but I knew that I was a real pain in the eighth grade. My home life was awful and I often lashed out in class. Mr. Baker said he did not remember it that way, though. Mr. Baker knew that I was having trouble at home. Anyone who would have walked into the room my eighth grade year would have known it. My hair was uncut, my clothes were dirty, and I am sure I did not smell that great. Still, Mr. Baker's room was a place of solitude where I forgot about all of the challenges outside of school. He was funny. He was firm, but I respected him. I could tell he cared about me and about all his students.

Weekends

As I have mentioned earlier, I spent as many weekends as I could away from my house. I went to many of my friends' homes and eventually wore out my welcome. I would ride my bike as far as I needed just to not be at home. Looking back, I can imagine why they got tired of me.

Generally speaking, we were underfed at my house, and so when I went to other people's houses I would eat and eat and eat. As I got older, I got hungrier. I would sleep over at Billy Wyatt's house, and I remember he and I would eat a dozen eggs for breakfast. I would go to my best friend Scott's house, but his parents rarely let me stay, I guess because they knew the damage I could do to the pantry while I was there after school, and were frightened what I might do if I slept over.

I also went to my friend Scott Holland's place. He lived about 12 miles away and I used to ride my bike there. We would get into all kinds of mischief. I remember we would ride our bikes to the drive-in movie theatre in Shelby. It was called the Sunset and must have been 11 or 12 miles away. We would ride our bikes on the country road because there were no lights, and then try to sneak in and watch the movie. If it was still light when we went we would try and collect returnable soda bottles along the way and get our 10-cent refund. We would buy firecrackers and candy with the money. We had so much fun together. Scott's parents drank as well, but they were not abusive. They were happy and fun-loving people.

If I ended up having to stay at my house on the weekend, it would usually just be my siblings and me with John and my mother, who would have their own private parties. They would blast country music outside to their special drinking area where they had set up a makeshift surround sound system. We had all gone to the drive-in movie theatre a few times, and each time the movie had finished, John would take wire cutters to one of the large waterproof speakers. He snipped the wires and stuffed it in the trunk, while my mom was in the driver's seat. We crammed in the backseat, with the motor running ready for the getaway. Back at the trailer, they set them up outside and ran a cable from the indoor speakers to these outdoor ones. It is amazing the lengths people will go to when they really believe in an idea, right or not.

Of course, on any given night, they would drink until way past the point they should have stopped. The situation can only be described as dysfunctional. They would start off being happy drinking, but ultimately it would lead to yelling, cursing and something getting broken. I remember trying to sleep while this was going on, but I would have to put a pillow around my ears the music was so loud.

During this time, John would continue to come in and molest my brother and me after my mother would pass out.

Back to Sroufe

The abuse at home would eventually reach a crescendo, but even though I had reached my early teens, I was still too small physically to fight back.

Mentally, though, I had begun to muster the courage that Mrs. Bailey had told me about. It was not until I started ninth grade at East Rutherford High School, though, that I decided I would reclaim who I really was.

One day, seemingly out of nowhere, I decided I was tired of being called Bill Kilgore when I knew my name was really William D. Sroufe. Therefore, I walked into Mr. Beason, the guidance counselor's office, and asked if it would be possible to make an appointment.

Mr. Beason, not knowing what he was in for, shrugged. "I can see you now if you have time."

I sat down and told my story, the whole story, while Mr. Beason listened with a deep commitment, and a look of disbelief. I explained, in detail, about the years of abuse, the terror, the beatings, the malcontent lifestyle.

I finished with, "I am not Bill Kilgore. My name is William David Sroufe."

After a brief moment of respite, he replied clearly, "I think I am going to need to speak to your mother." I immediately went home to tell my mother what had happened. I found her in the cramped hallway of the trailer and explained to her the conversation I had just had with the guidance counselor.

I declared, "I want to change my name back to what it always should have been. I am a Sroufe. NOT a Kilgore."

My mother began yelling at me. "You are so ungrateful!! John has done nothing but love you! Your father abandoned you, and this is the thanks we get."

She smacked me across the face, hard. I retreated to my room and moved the dresser in front of the door. My mother stood in the hall yelling for what seemed an eternity. I stayed in my room for the rest of the night, not even coming out for dinner. I slept on the floor, wedging myself between my bed and the dresser so no one could get in.

The next day, with scratches from my mom's fingernails across my face, I went back to the counselor's office. I explained to Mr. Beason what had occurred, but he said the only way he could change my name was to speak with my mother and that he would need a birth certificate.

I went back to my mother after school. Surprised by my own courage, I told her that the counselor needed to see her and that she was to bring my birth certificate with her. She just picked up on the same conversation, the same screaming about my ungratefulness.

However, I held my ground. "John has been good to me? Are you kidding?!" I screamed. "He has molested me for years and you know it! What have you done to protect me from him?"

The sound of my own voice was deafening in the small space.

"You have done nothing!!" I continued. "This is a miserable life that you have created and I don't want any part of it anymore. I do not want any part of you. I do not want any part of John Kilgore.

I took a deep breath and with unwavering fortitude, I announced, "My name is William David Sroufe, and I will go back every day to Mr. Beason's office until he calls you or you call him."

My mother just stared at me. Then she went into her room.

I heard her shuffling through papers until finally she returned and threw my birth certificate at me.

"I hope you're happy," she said and walked away.

The next day I went to see Mr. Beason again, and much to his surprise, presented him with my birth certificate. I am not sure if he was surprised that I had been telling the truth or that I had gotten the proof I needed.

Regardless, it was the most empowering moment of my life thus far.

Throughout the day, I went around proudly explaining to each of my teachers and all of my friends my name change.

Little did I know this was just the beginning of something.

Leaving

To this day, I am not sure why Mr. Beason did not call social services after I told him everything; I guess because it was a different time. I knew other kids who were beaten by their parents, who lived in squalor, but you never heard about social services being called in or the kids being taken away from their parents back then. Maybe he did call someone and they did nothing, maybe he did not, but regardless, I knew what I had to do.

I had finally grown tired of the escalating abuse, the deplorable lifestyle.

There is a saying that if a frog is thrown into a boiling pot of water it will immediately jump out to save itself, but if you put it in cool water and slowly heat the water to boiling, the frog will die before it realizes what has happened. This is so often what happens with abusive relationships, but for some reason, I knew if I stayed in this boiling pot of water that was my home life, I would die.

For a few months, I had been calling my father collect, telling him about what was going on. A week after I told him I changed my name back to Sroufe, he said he was coming to see me. He had planned trips before that had never transpired, but this time he actually came.

He arrived on Saturday morning and picked Lisa, Ralph and I up at the trailer and took us to breakfast. We spent the whole day together and it was incredible. We went to a movie, and then out for lunch. He even took us to buy some clothes at the local mall. I almost felt normal, or what I thought normal should be. That night, he stayed at a motel, while we went back to the trailer. When he dropped us off, he spoke to my mother and John without us in the room but never told me what they talked about. He had been friends with John years earlier, and although he and my mother had divorced long before, I am sure it was still awkward.

He picked us up on a Sunday morning and we went out for breakfast again. Eating out was such a rarity that it seems to be the thing I remember most about the visit. It really was such a treat to be treated. Then he dropped us back off at the trailer again. I remember the conversation on the dirt and gravel driveway before he left to return home to Norfolk. He told me that he would contact a lawyer about me maybe coming to live with him. I remember Ralph sitting on the trunk of his Buick Skyhawk as we took pictures. It had been such a good weekend, after a tumultuous week, and there seemed to be some hope in a hopeless world.

The last thing he asked me was, "Are you okay? What do you want to do?"

"I want to leave here," I shrugged. "I have to leave here."

He promised he was going to talk with an attorney as soon as he got home.

The next week went as normal. By then everyone knew about my name change. It felt so good. Like I was wearing fresh clothes. Friday came like other Fridays, though, and I still had not heard from my dad. I went to the football game, as I did whenever they had a home game. As always, I stayed as late as I could, until the last possible ride, I could catch to drive me home was leaving.

It was late when I arrived at the trailer, and my mother and John were drunk. I headed straight for my room, but she stopped me.

In a drunken rant, my mother began to berate me, "You are just like your father! You are worthless. You think changing your name is going to mean something?" She laughed viciously. "You will never become anything!"

I came back at her, "What? You think I want to be like you? A drunk? Married to a drunk! What do you have? What have you done? You have allowed this man to abuse us, to beat us, to molest us! What kind of mother are you?"

John came out of his chair, stumbling toward me, but I escaped into my room. I pushed the dresser in front of the door and wedged myself between the dresser and the bed again. The hallway was too small for him to leverage any force, besides he was so drunk he was like a noodle.

I slept there all night.

Saturday morning came quickly and I remember being sore from sleeping wedged between the hard furniture. I had done it many times before to protect myself, but there was something different about this morning. I got up and bolted out of the house before anyone got up. I wandered along the railroad tracks, ending up at Scott's house. We spent the day just hanging out but never talked about what was happening at my house. I suspect Scott knew it was not great, but he never knew the details. I still never wanted to tell him or anyone, because I was scared I would have no friends if they knew the truth. Even though it was not something I had done, I was ashamed. In addition, while I was away from home I wanted to be fully in that environment and not even think about what was going on at home.

Later that afternoon, Scott had to get ready for a movie date, so I went to my friend Michael's house and we wandered in the woods. He taught me how to navigate through some dense places I had never been before.

Finally, around dark, I went home.

My life had become one horrific Ground Hog Day, so I was

not surprised when I arrived to find my mother drunk. She instantly dove into the same berating as the night before, but this time my sister was there and joined in. They teamed up in their degrading and belittling of me, echoing insults about my father.

I tried to avoid the 'conversation' by going straight to my room, but my mother was following quickly behind me. She started hitting me in the back of the head, but I would not stop so she dug her nails into my shoulders; so hard that I bled into my shirt. I was in shock, but I remember being most upset that she was ruining the yellow OP shirt that Scott had given me.

Angry, I turned around, but before I could say anything, she slapped me across the face. Then grabbing me by the shoulders, she yelled incoherently into my face. I am not sure why, but my mother had an extremely strong grip, especially when she was in this erratic state.

Finally, I had had enough and pried her hands off me. John came in behind me screaming, but then my mother turned on him.

"This is all your fault! You have abused him and beat him. You're to blame!!"

She went to hit him with her clenched fists, but he grabbed her by the hands and held them back. I rushed into my room, returning with a sawed-off shovel handle I had in my room. I hit him over the head with it - hard enough that he stumbled into the hallway and fell down. My mother gasped and went to his side, but, unfortunately, he was only stunned. I went back in my room, slammed the door and pushed the dresser in front of it, again wedging myself between the dresser and the bed.

My mother screamed that I was grounded and then I heard them both go back into the living room. I decided then, I could not live like this anymore. I waited there wedged in my room.

I waited for them to continue drinking. I waited for my moment.

Eventually, it came.

After about an hour, I heard their bedroom door shut. I listened for silence.

Then I put on my shoes and slowly moved the dresser out of the way. I slipped quietly out the back door and down the dirt road. I did not take a thing except the clothes on my back.

I would never return to my mother's house. In many ways, I would never let her return to my life.

I worked my way through a path in the woods that Michael had, coincidently, just shown me that afternoon. I snuck behind my grandparents' house and got on the railroad tracks that led to Scott's house. As I walked down the tracks, I realized that Scott probably still was not home from his date yet. I knew I could not go to my grandparents' house, so I decided on the Stampers, who were some neighboring friends.

Jody Stamper, the dad, answered the door and I was crying. Eyes full of compassion, he said, "Come in, come in."

He never asked what was wrong. He did not have to. He knew about my situation at home. Everyone did.

I remember Jody was not feeling well, but I do not recall where his wife, Pat, or their daughters, Kristie and Michelle, were. I tried calling my father, who was now a psychologist, but all I had was his office number. It may sound foolish now, but I did not even know I could call information to get the number.

Jody and I just sat for a while and watched TV. His wife and daughters still were not home when I went to bed.

The next morning, I woke up very early to find Pat frying sausage and eggs. She offered me some, but I was too nervous to eat. The first thing I did was call Scott.

Scott answered, "Your mom called looking for you."

"I'm not going back there, Scott. Ever." I had never been more serious in my life. "Can you come get me?"

"Of course. I'll borrow my dad's truck."

I got off the phone not having any clue what I was going to do, but I thanked the Stampers and left. Although this wonderful family granted me sanctuary on this life-changing night, I would never see them again. However, I will never forget them and the kindness they showed me.

I walked down the road where I met up with Scott. He drove us back to his place. His parents listened to what had happened and recommended I call my father, but I told them I did not have his number. Mrs. Hoppes suggested calling information in Norfolk. I remembered the name of the hospital where my father worked, so-called the answering service. Within ten minutes, he called me back.

I explained what had happened, and he asked, "What do you want to do?" "Come live with you!"

"Where is the closest airport?"

"Charlotte, about an hour from us." "Can Scott's parents take you?"

Scott and I answered for them, but my father asked to speak to them. Mr. Hoppes very generously, said, "Yes. Of course."

Mrs. Hoppes asked Scott to get me a coat and another pair of shoes, as I had left with only a shirt and my runners were worn through.

We hopped in the truck, and Scott's parents drove the 60 miles to take me to Charlotte. After ten years of hell, it was all arranged so quickly and by midday, I was boarding a plane to go live with my dad.

I was terrified and relieved.

I have written the Hoppes' over the years and even sent them a copy of my dissertation because without them I could not have done it. Without them, I would have stayed living in hell.

The plane landed in Norfolk, Virginia mid-afternoon, and my dad was there to meet me. We went for lunch in the Ghent District where we met Leo, my father's AA sponsor and long-time friend, and Linda, his girlfriend. We went to a restaurant on Colley Avenue named The Intermission and I had 'Stuffed Hunk of Steak'. My father later recalled how quickly I ate, comparing me to a prisoner of war. Which is exactly how I had felt the ten years prior. Now I was free.

After lunch, we went to my father's third-floor apartment on Gates Ave.

He had a galley kitchen and I remember standing in there with him when he called my grandparents. I have never been so nervous. My father and grandparents had always gotten along as far as I knew, but I still was not sure how they would react to the news I had just run away, flown away, to live with him.

My father asked me to step into the living room while he spoke with my grandfather. I anxiously waited as I heard the muffled conversation behind the doors. Initially, I was afraid that my father was wanting to send me back to Ellenboro, or that there would be some legal trouble and I would have to go back.

After what seemed an eternity, I heard my father say, "Alright."

Then the kitchen doors opened and he asked, "Can you come in here, Bill?

Your grandfather would like to talk to you."

My heart sank. I had just done one of the most courageous things, but I was still worried my grandfather would be disappointed in me. My father handed me the phone and both my grandparents were on the line. They told me that it would be okay. "If this is what you want, Bill, we will support you."

I was so relieved. I hung up the phone feeling as if everything would be okay.

Then my father called my mother.

At first, I could hear my mother crying through the phone line, and evidently, John was on the line. Though I could not hear the words, they were saying I could derive from my father's answers that they were threatening my father with some sort of legal action. My father remained calm but firm. He simply told them he knew of the abuse. He knew of the drinking and the callous disregard for my wellbeing, and I told him that day about the abuse I was enduring from John and if they wanted to seek legal action, he would gladly contact an attorney. John got off the phone, and the tone of my father's voice softened. He asked my mother if she would like to speak to me. He handed me the phone, and my mother began to cry and yell at me. I cannot remember what I said if I said anything. This conversation ended quickly.

I was 400 miles away. I was safe, finally safe.

(Not the) Final Chapter

I would like to say that this was the end of a tumultuous life, but in some ways, it was just the beginning - still I would not have done anything differently. There were many events after I came to live with my dad. Being a single parent was all so new to him. He has passed on now, and I love and miss him every day, but he was not the greatest father in the world because I do not think he knew how to be.

When I first came to live with him, we shared an apartment with two other people and he was always so worried about me. It is hard to explain, but I guess the best way to describe it is to say he constantly looked after me.

He would follow me around and say, "Are you okay, Bill? Do you need anything?"

I was not used to anyone caring where I was or what I was doing, so this level of attention felt smothering. It is as if I had been transported to a different world; we definitely both experienced some culture shock. I went to Norfolk Catholic High School and a friend of his, Sister Jean, worked there and must have been given some sort of orders from my dad because she treated me the same way at school. Part of the overprotectiveness, I am sure, was due to guilt, but there were also no parenting books back then and he went from being alone to raising a teenage son with barely a week's notice.

My dad immediately took me to a doctor for a physical. I had not seen an eye doctor or a dentist since Mrs. Bailey had sent me in the 6th grade, so he took me to see them as well.

He also spoiled me. Knowing the lack I had lived with up until then, it is understandable that he wanted to shower me in gifts, but I also think, like is so often the case with men, this was his way of expressing his love for me. I had this affinity for the color blue, and so my dad decorated my room in blue—blue sheets, a blue chair, and blue lampshade. I even had my own telephone number, and my phone was blue.

He would buy me clothes, take me to movies and gave me about a $100 a week for allowance. Having spent an entire weekend scrounging around for 25 cents only a couple years before, this was a fortune to me. I am not sure how long this lasted, but I remember one thing I would do with the money is sent roses to girls I liked. I also took friends to the movies and went to a number of concerts, like Jefferson Starship, A-ha, Bruce Springsteen, U2, Night Ranger and Phil Collins. It felt so good to be experiencing life.

It had only been a couple of months earlier that I was sitting on my bed in my tiny room in that disgusting trailer. The heat was off and we had no food. I remember thinking to myself, *I've got to do something different. I can't live like this anymore.*

Again, children should not have to think like this and at the time, I did not know what I was going to do. I did not know my dad was going to come around and that I would be able to take advantage of him being a father again.

However, here we were. Moreover, I could finally be a kid.

The other part of the story is that he and his father never got along. His father, a career Navy man, was an alcoholic. He died in 1982 and my dad did not even go to his funeral.

Although my dad eventually went to university to become a psychologist, he had actually never graduated high school. The story goes that after he quit, my grandmother paid some principal in North Carolina to get him a diploma.

My dad was always this really thin guy, so I can imagine how small he was as a teenager. He used to lie about his age all the time but somehow got away with it. I remember him telling me about one year when The World's Fair was in New York City my dad went out and got a job as a guide. He was 15 years old.

I guess what I am saying is he had to grow up fast. He raised himself in lots of different ways and made some mistakes. And here I was, having just run away. He knew what I had been through and was very precautionary about everything.

He was also a licensed psychologist. Need I say more?

Thanksgiving Visit

I left Ellenboro the first week of November and as far as I can remember the only conversation I had had with my mother was on the phone in the kitchen the day I arrived at my dad's, but we would see each other face-to-face the following Thanksgiving. It was not typical to travel on holidays, but I guess because I had moved to Norfolk, my mother and John decided to come up and visit his mother for the long weekend.

My mother had called my father and asked if I could be dropped off at John's mother's house on Friday, but he explained to her that it was my decision and that he would discuss it with me and get back with her. I do not know how he did it, but my dad never talked poorly about my mother. Ever the therapist, he took me aside and told me about the phone call he had had with her, and wanted to know how I felt about it. My immediate reaction was—no way. I was scared to death about the entire prospect, but my dad, in a roundabout way, said it might be the right thing to do.

So, on a Friday morning, he took me to John's mother's house on Robin Hood Road in Norfolk. He told me to call if he was needed, but that my mother would bring me home otherwise.

As soon as I entered the house, my mother began crying. My brother and half-sister were there, and so were John's grandfather and mother.

My mother did not waste any time before tearing into me. "So, are you coming back with us to Ellenboro?" She demanded to know.

I calmly replied, "No. I am not. And I do not want to talk about it. I just came to see you and Ralph and Leigh Anne."

Nevertheless, she kept on me. She started criticizing me about why I wanted to live with my father. "You just want to live with him because he's rich," she claimed. "John has provided for you for years while your father didn't even care about you!"

I shot back. "No, you took me away to another state and didn't tell him until we were there. You allowed John to abuse Ralph and me, and you are still defending him right now. I left because I am not a Kilgore. I am a Sroufe, and I will always be a Sroufe. I left to escape a crazy and chaotic house, full of lies and deceit."

The tension was palpable; finally, I asked if I could be taken home. John piped in, "You're staying!"

"No, John. I'm not." I stood up, "I'm either gonna call my father or the police or walk home myself unless someone takes me!"

My mother began yelling and crying, begging me to stay. I exclaimed I would not. It started to grow more chaotic as everyone was yelling, screaming or crying.

Finally, my mother agreed. John's mother really did not live that far from my dad's place, but I can ensure you it was an agonizingly long ride. I sat quietly as my mother drove. As she got closer to our apartment building I could feel my heart pounding, and I nearly jumped from the slow-moving car.

We lived in a secured building and I remember hopping out of the car, running to the door, punching in the code, rushing in and quickly securing the door behind me.

Once again, I felt relieved.

My father was home, and I caught him off guard. I began crying and told him I never wanted to do that again. He just hugged me.

Back to Virginia Beach

The summer after I left North Carolina, before entering the tenth grade, we moved to Virginia Beach where my father went into private practice at Atlantic Psychiatric Services.

We lived in a condominium, and I started writing poetry again. My father was a bit more open, so I never hid my poems from him. I remember writing "the world between" and leaving it in the living room. He discovered it and was really upset. He was not mad at me; he was afraid for me.

the world between
lying so close to the future
in a place where dreams are past
present is an existence of still images
dark within a laugh
my tears are crying loudly
my heart stops once again
what seems like forever – was
and will never return again
it's not a story of sadness
yet I have dreamt it once before
i'm caught within the future
of a hundred thousand more
if I sing a song of laughter
i would just be living a lie
so I close my eyes to wonder
and breathe so deeply to die

Fearing I was contemplating suicide, my dad made me go into counseling for about a year. I remember going to two different therapists, but Dr. Thomas Tsao, the first one, was the one I remember most. He was a very nice man, and on the first day, said to me, "So why are you here?"

I think I laughed and said my father was making me. Dr. Tsao led me through different processes, guiding me with questions. I do not remember the details or even the name of the second therapist, I just remember I would go and talk about whatever was bothering me. Still, I never felt safe enough to talk about what happened with John. In fact, for years, I would not even say his name, but only refer to him as "my mother's husband," and when someone would say he was my stepfather, I quickly corrected them.

It was not all serious, though. As it was the summer when we first arrived, I quickly discovered the joy of sailing. My father had a 37-foot sailboat, which I absolutely loved. Her name was *Easy Does It*—a slogan of sorts from AA. We would often go storm sailing together. We both loved the excitement and had more than one adventure on her.

One Saturday afternoon, I remember, we decided to head out from our slip at Waterside in Norfolk. The trip up the Elizabeth River went by the Norfolk Naval Shipyard, the largest Naval base in the world. My father and I both had an affinity for submarines. My grandfather, my father's dad, was a career Navy man and spent all but his first year on diesel submarines, so perhaps it was genetic.

On this day, we saw there was a large submarine in port and so both wanted to see it up close. I was steering the boat up the river, so maneuvered in very close so we could get a good look. The Navy seaman was none too happy to see us, though.

He came to the edge of the retaining rope and waved us off, and then he pointed his M-16 at us. We followed his direction to not get so close and continued up the river. A few minutes later, while my father was down below making coffee, a light started flashing behind me. It was a Coast Guard cutter.

The next thing I heard was a deep voice bellow, "Heave to and prepare for a boarding party!"

Just as my father was coming up, the cutter came up beside *Easy Does It* and a Coast Guard officer saluted and asked, "Captain, permission to come aboard?"

My father saluted him back and said, "Permission granted."

The cutter left and the Coasties explained they had boarded because we had gotten so close to the submarine, and it was uncharacteristic of someone to get so close. They then conducted an inspection. I remember watching my father from outside of the conversation. I always had so much respect for him, how he carried himself, how he spoke, and this was no different. He was explaining to the Coastguardsmen about his father's service in the US Navy and having served on submarines, and me being part of his life. The men listened as they drank a cup of coffee and carried out their inspection.

My father did get fined for having no flares, though.

The summer of my junior year, my father, uncle and I sailed up the Chesapeake Bay to Baltimore. I think it took about two weeks. I remember sitting down with my father and planning each day. We planned the meals and what port we were going to stop at and stay overnight. I remember we ate really good food and enjoyed our evenings immensely at each port along the Chesapeake Bay. My father was a foodie and loved to cook. The boat had its challenges as we did not have an electric refrigerator, so each night in port we would go and get bags of ice.

When we arrived in Baltimore, we explored the city, and we were able to visit the *USS Torsk*, an old diesel submarine that my father's father served on in 1946-47. Each port was different, and while I do not recall the entire journey, I do remember that we spent a lot of time together.

As we sat in ports or sailed along on our journey we would listen to music, stop for a swim, or my father and I would have debates about the existence of God.

My father was a man of faith, but I have always struggled with faith because of my life, and the way of the world. This debate would go on and on as I would pose questions to him about the state of the world or even the things that happened to me.

He would start quoting things to me about faith: "Mother Teresa said, 'Be faithful in small things because it is in them that your strength lies.'"

"Dad, how can small things bring me faith?" I would ask then he would quote the Bible.

"In 1 Thessalonians 2:13 it says, 'And we also thank God continually because, when you received the word of God, which you heard from us, you accepted it not as a human word, but as it actually is, the word of God, which is indeed at work in you who believe.' So it is not me telling you to have faith, it is God. It is God's word."

And I would ask again, "How do you know?"

"I know because I have faith." And then my father would say:

"In Revelations 21:4 it says 'There will come a day when God will wipe every tear from our eyes and there will be no more death or mourning or crying or pain, for the old order of things will pass away.' He proved that by sending His only Son. There is no greater sacrifice," my father added.

The truth is I have struggled with faith on many different levels. I still struggle with faith as an adult. I know God is with me. I simply look at my children and I know. But I cannot explain the evil in the world, and not just what happened to me. But I guess that is where faith lies for most people. I pray. Still, faith is something I struggle with every day.

Ultimately, I would always ask the same question of my father. "Can you prove to me that God exists?"

And he would always give me the same answer. "Can you prove to me He doesn't?"

I never had a clear answer for him, and I guess I still do not.

Lessons in Love

In the fall, I began attending Floyd E. Kellam High School and on the first day, while in study hall, I sat across from a beautiful girl. I spotted her again later in the cafeteria and started talking to her. Her name was Angela Champion.

School got a whole lot more interesting on that day. I thought it was destiny that we had met as her father was from Forest City, NC, just one town over from Ellenboro. We started dating, and if I know what love is, I would say that I loved her.

We dated for a while but eventually broke up as many teenagers do. I wrote a poem for her called "dying heart".

dying heart
the dying heart bleeds with passion the person letting go
was not as easy as it would seem the destiny between the two
had not been the same as intended now reality had struck
with a cruel memory of heartache to believe in something
so unbelievable
to have lived something so unreal
now in present time using logic
confusing enough it seemed
but now it looked to have no hope informally i asked
informally she declined without a destine of solitude i listened
*   to her answer*
without regret of being embarrassed, i asked again
with a pause in conversation that seemed tense
she smiled …
staring at her beautiful eyes that expression was told before be-
*   coming truth*
i took her hand

squeezed it gently to let her know i cared she gave in
the memories flashed back had she changed?
had i?
would we be the same? i thought "no"
only with hope will we have a chance but now i recognize
the feelings seem mutual
the night passes, we move on the love scene plays in my head i
*   catch a fragrance; her perfume*
the attraction that leads me to her in the darkest of nights
i run to her; fighting my way every inch through this life
and as she turned to my call
i took her in my arms and without hesitation, i kissed her
and as she returned my kiss
i thought what was running through her mind?
i asked without regret
she answered without hesitation i love you
as the tears fell from my eyes i said i love you, too
then …
i seemed to rub something from my eyes
sleep, sandman dust, from the night before
i had been dreaming
i jumped into and out of a dream i had been asleep
the dying heart bleeds with passion where to find it?
where did it go? where will it end?

Near the end of our junior year, I began dating another girl, Christina Travis, but she had already promised her friend that she would go to the Ring Dance with him. We talked about it, and I agreed she should uphold her promise and so I had decided not to go. A week or so before the dance, Angie called me crying and upset because something happened with her date for the Ring Dance, and she was wondering if I would take her. I agreed and the next day went and rented a black tux.

We shared a limo with Anne Walker and Sean Scott. It was fun, but when we got to the dance we both went our separate ways. Eventually, we met up again and danced a bit.

At the end of the night, we rode back home in the limo together. Angela had had a little too much to drink, so the ride back was a little more exciting than the ride out. Loving someone and sharing your time together is so important, even if it does not last forever. Christina and I did not go out much longer after that, and Angie and I never got back together.

The following year, around November, my friend Todd and I snuck into a movie at Lynnhaven Mall. It was *White Nights* starring Mikhail Baryshnikov and Gregory Hines. The theatre was full, so they asked everyone to move in to fill all the empty center seats. As fate would have it, I again sat next to a beautiful girl. We started chatting and when the movie ended, I walked her and her cousin through Belk, a local department store, to catch her ride. I got her phone number and we soon began calling one another. She had told me upfront that her family would be moving to Hawaii in March as her father was in the Navy, but I did not care.

It was a typical high school love story, short and passionate. In the few months we dated, I do not think we disagreed about anything. We made plans to see each other that summer, but they never happened.

When I went to the airport to see her off in March, I gave her a poem I had written for her:

april
we will not see an April yesterday has no spring
no May within our memory
it's only March within our dreams
we've had no long-lost summers
no sunsets at the beach
thunderstorms don't come in November
it's only March within our dreams
we have the decorations
the moment that we met
the silence of holding hands
all the time we spent together or apart
time has mattered not
it's March within our dreams
perhaps I will dream tomorrow

Girls seemed to be my major in high school or at the very least, my main interest as I dated a few other girls along the way. The summer of 1987, after graduation, a high school friend of mine introduced me to a girl who was working at McDonald's in Lynnhaven Mall. She was a beautiful blonde-haired girl with blue eyes. I thought she was entirely out of my league, but asked her what time she got off work anyways. There was a back hallway in the mall and so I waited back there for her to come out. I was leaning against the wall when she exited the back door to McDonald's and I caught her off guard. She seemed nervous because she kept fixing her hair with her hand. Of course, I thought that meant she did not want to talk to me, and so I asked her why she was so grumpy.

That encounter started a beautiful relationship. Lori and I were inseparable for three years. She had been an only child until her junior year of high school when her mother got pregnant with twin girls. We used to babysit the girls all the time. Still, I remember her parents were the first parents who seemed not like me. Perhaps it was them being protective of her, but they always kept me at a distance whenever possible. It was a quintessential love story that could have been taken from fairytales, but some things are not meant to be. Lori Francisco helped define me as a man. We were teenage lovers and like so many young people could not juggle the monstrous task of being in love with all of the other complications of life. Still, she taught me how to trust, and how to love. She helped me strengthen the courage that Mrs. Bailey helped me find; she always believed in me—

who I was and who I would become. I guess in the end I was still broken. She tried her best to straighten me out, but we just could not make it work.

the road away
in between and behind a segment of time
a regret in the cornerstone of my muse
the yesterday of the yesterday
i've dreamt years since
i would wonder where you went
on the road away
i've found your memory
traveling the course of time
life continued in the parallel
dreaming of different days
on the road ahead
i sought your memory
your heart is still in place
in between the roads, it resides

between yesterday and today
falling footprints
left too far a distance
things I've yet to say
fallen in the epic journey
on the road away
yesterday brought me here
those memories have faded to the past
still, share time with today
and exist on the road away

Music

If girls had been my major in high school, then music would have been my minor. I just loved the words and the flow. I was never musically talented, and to this day I still cannot sing, but I love to anyways. With all the struggles, chaos and uncertainty in my life over the years, the one thing I could always rely upon was music.

Early on it was listening to AM radio in the evening alone in my room.

There were times in the winter when my mother and her husband only heated the living room with a single heater in order to save money. The walls of trailers in the early 80s were thin, so I would have to bury myself under the covers to keep warm. Cuddled beneath, music took me places, fantastic dreamlike places. I would often stay up late into the night anticipating the next song that would come on the radio. It could have been the raspy voice of Bob Seger or KISS or Jackson Brown, it did not matter, and somehow it always made my world better.

I listened to FM radio on the weekends, counting down the top hits with Casey Kasem all the while trying to sift through the new sounds of Prince, Grand Master Flash and the Furious 5, David Bowie, Van Halen or Air Supply.

I remember singing to Alabama, Ronnie Milsap, and Rod Stewart. It did not matter what happened to me or where I was I could always count on the Eagles or The Bee Gees to help me escape my own thoughts. I could hide away in the words of a song, feeling not so alone because someone else had experienced some of the same heartaches I had. The evil that leeched onto my life and into my path could easily disappear as the music took its place.

I remember my old 8-track tape player only had one speaker, but I had an ABBA tape and a few greatest hits tapes. I wore the player out, eventually taking it apart to see what was wrong. I was able to have my grandfather help me replace a small belt, and solder a wire or two to get it back into operation.

When I went to live with my father, the first thing I would do when I came home from school was put on *The Eagles Greatest Hits Volume 2*. I remember every pop and crack on that album. I must have listened to "New Kid in Town" 10,000 times. I could not help but relate to the words: "Great expectations, everybody's watching you. People you meet, they all seem to know you…"

It was as if Henley, Frey, and Souther wrote the song about me.

My love affair music has never sauntered. I can recall a U.N. mission I went on while in the Air Force. I went to Nairobi, Kenya, and Mwanza, Tanzania during the Rwanda Relief Effort. I took my Sony Walkman, and one tape: *The Eagles: Their Greatest Hits 1971-1975*. I would sit in a cargo net and listen to the entire album over and over again.

It was hard not to identify with Don Mclean when he wrote the song "American Pie" and how one day the music died.

The truth for me is that music has helped identify who I am—from the words of Dave Matthew to Keith Urban. Even the words of the boy band One Direction, who were introduced to me by my daughter, explain the story of my life:

"written in these walls are the stories that I can't explain"

Maybe that is why I love music—I am trying to find the words to explain what has happened, and what will happen.

High School Teachers

Although once I left Ellenboro, I had my dad as a positive adult influence in my life, and was extremely grateful for him; there was definitely something, or someone, missing. My elementary school teachers had had such an impact on my life that I think the nature of high school, especially in a large city, left a void. In fact, there were only really three teachers who I felt a connection with: Mr. Boyd, my history teacher; Mrs. Wadsworth, my eleventh grade English teacher; and Mrs. Jackson, my twelfth grade English teacher. I had a few other teachers I remember, but not fondly. Mostly because of the self-doubt they created in me.

My journalism teacher, Ms. Adams, for example, clearly did not think a lot of me as a student. This especially bothered me as I had such a passion for writing. She had her favorites and I remember asking her one time why she consistently chose this one particular student over me when giving out tasks for the newspaper.

She would simply reply, "Because they are a better writer than you."

"Well, how am I going to get better if I'm never given any assignments?"

That response didn't garner any more opportunities, but years later, after I got out of the Air Force and was working on my undergraduate degree, I worked at Kinko's doing desktop publishing. One day, Ms. Adams came in. I recognized her immediately, but she did not know who I was until I prompted her. Once she realized I was a former student, she acted interested and wondered what I was doing with my life.

"I just got out of the Air Force."

"Oh yeah, how was that?"

"Great. I was a journalist for them and editor of the paper. Also, I am currently writing for the Chesapeake Bureau of *The Pilot*, while I am going to school to become a teacher."

She stared at me and just said "Congratulations!" And then went on her way.

I found a little justice in telling her what I had been able to accomplish. I knew I was not going to win a Pulitzer Prize, but I had been recognized as the 1992 United States Air Forces in Europe Public Affairs Airmen of the Year. I did not tell her all that, but inside I knew that I wanted to be a different teacher than she was to me. I wanted to lift kids up instead of bringing them down. Give them opportunities, instead of keeping them stuck.

As I have mentioned, I started writing poetry at fourteen, but it was not until I got to Kellam High School that I finally had the courage to show someone besides my dad. I began showing them to girls and a few close friends, and then I decided I would show it to a new teacher I had. I thought to myself, *She is young and will understand me.*

I still have the handwritten poem that she critiqued to the point of destruction. Wow! I never knew how fast wind could be taken out of someone's sails. Still, I pressed on and was eventually able to convince myself that hers was just one perspective. I also kept the poem, I guess to remember the value I find in myself. I would learn over the coming years that some people would not find the value in my words; in fact, no one would find them as valuable as me and that was okay. Giving me the poem with all the corrections gave me strength not only as a writer but also a teacher. It takes strength for a young man to write poetry and share it. Still, the teacher only found things to critique, so by keeping it I could remind myself that there is always room to grow, and also stop sometimes before I critique and compliment—to always question what good will come out of my words.

It was in Virginia Beach that I had decided I wanted to become a professional writer, so started down the path taking courses in high school. I took Advanced Writers Composition and my teacher was Ms. Bryan. It was a small class compared to my others, probably no more than 15 students.

It was in this class that I gained more than just confidence in my writing; I gained perspective on how to overcome obstacles in life. I remember the first day of class vividly. As soon as Ms. Bryan started teaching us, I thought to myself, *There is no way she can do this.*

You see, Ms. Bryan had Parkinson's disease. She stammered and stuttered as she spoke, but by the end of the class I did not even notice; she was one of the most fascinating people I had ever known. She would tell us stories about her youth, which I guess was how she created a connection with us. She told us how she had hung out with the rock group The Who and how they had once "drank Kool-Aid all night long."

She was funny but also had high expectations for us. Her critiques of my writing were always constructive and I knew their intention was to help me grow as a writer. She never once brought me down, but she continuously lifted me up. She wanted me to become the best writer I could be.

Ms. Bryan really did help me with my writing, but as for my other subjects? It is lucky I had my father's support at home. He never put me down or doubted what I could do. He would tell me that a "C" was acceptable and being average at some things was okay. Although this may seem like he was lowering his standards, he was not because somehow simultaneously he always made me feel like I could accomplish anything I set my mind on.

He also always told me he loved me, which is why I believed him.

Graduating into the Real World

I graduated from Floyd E. Kellam High School in 1987. As I mentioned, that summer, I had begun dating Lori and I also started college at Tidewater Community College while working at a Thom McAn Shoe Store in Lynnhaven Mall. This went on for a year, and although it was a busy time, everything seemed to be going smoothly in life. So I thought.

One Saturday that summer, I got up and went to the early morning monthly meeting at my work. When I returned my father and his third wife, Allison, were sitting at the breakfast table and asked me to come in and have a seat.

My father got to the point saying that I was, "18 now" and that he was giving me thirty days to find somewhere else to live, because things, "didn't seem to be working out."

I was totally blind-sided as I thought of myself as an extremely responsible young man. I did not drink and never stayed out late; I even made dinners and cleaned. I quickly went from bewildered to furious. I immediately called my girlfriend and then my friend Todd, whose mother said I could live there for a while if I wanted. I called my manager at work, told her what happened and asked for the day off to move.

As Todd and I were packing my stuff into my Isuzu truck, my father said, "You don't have to move out today. I'm giving you a month."

I said, "If you don't want me here, then I don't want to be here," and I continued packing my things. I have been on my own ever since.

My father and I did not speak for almost a year. But then there came a time when we both realized our relationship was important.

By then my father had started scuba diving. He dove all the time and got me hooked on it, too. He had his own private practice so was able to see patients on Friday and then take off to the Bahamas for the weekend. He became a master level instructor. I started teaching, too, but my earnings mostly went to pay for the expensive equipment.

I wanted to become a cop, but when the time came I could not pass the eye exam. Police officers could not have corrective lenses back then, a regulation I did not find out about for over a year.

So, I continued working in retail for a couple years, becoming the manager of the shoe store where I worked. It was okay, although the pay was not great so I was back to living hand to mouth. But then there came a moment when things flipped for me. I went to one of the regional manager's meetings and there was this 40 year-old manager there. He was a nice guy and I had worked with him for a few years, but I was doing what he was doing and I was not even 20!

I thought, *Damn, I don't wanna be doing this when I'm forty.*

In the coming days, I began talking to a friend of mine, Paul Dalenberg, about joining the military, in particular, the Air Force. Paul was an assistant manager at a Kentucky Fried Chicken restaurant and he was thinking about joining the military as well. We made an appointment and went to see a recruiter. We had heard there was a buddy system where two people could join together, but the recruiter told us it no longer existed. He advised us on what we should do to join and so we both scheduled ourselves to take the ASVAB, a multiple-aptitude battery of tests that measures developed abilities and helps predict future academic and occupational success in the military.

When our results came back, we scheduled our appointments together once again to talk to the recruiter about possible positions in the military. We both joined the Air Force on the spot with Paul going into the computer field and me into public affairs. We spent the coming weeks on a delayed enlistment waiting for our spot in basic training. While we waited, we would run and train with the recruiter knowing that we needed to be in better shape when we arrived in Texas in the coming weeks.

I remember my grandfather (my mother's father) telling me, "Either you will love it or hate it but at least it will send you in a direction. It will either motivate you to stay in and pursue a career in the service or motivate you to do something else."

And he was right. About all of it.

Some Things Change, and Some Things Stay the Same

After the Thanksgiving debacle, a few years would pass before I would see my mother and John again. My best friend, Jeff Mitchell, was a pilot, so one time we rented a plane and flew to Greensboro. Supposedly, my mother had stopped drinking, and she and John were running a furniture factory.

We landed at the airport and then, using the courtesy car, drove to their house. Neither my mother nor John was there, but John's brother Doug was and he had a Jeep, which he let me drive while we were waiting for them to return. My brother took Jeff and me to the "factory", which was no more than a cinder block building with a sign and pieces of unassembled wooden furniture strewn about. We did not stay very long and by the time we got back to the house, they were there.

And my mother was so drunk she could not stand up.

I was devastated by the visit. I was embarrassed that I had Jeff there with me to witness the chaos. I was still so naive about my mother and her drinking. I would constantly make up these stories in my head about her getting better, that she would finally stop drinking and leave John. I was mad at myself for believing her and making the trip. I was finally safe and did not need her in my life, but I let her back in and she betrayed me. It is a sickening experience when your own mother betrays you—betrays your trust.

The continued mistrust lasted for a few years; I decided that I did not even want to speak with her. My father would ask me from time to time, "Have you spoken with your mother?"

"No."

"You know, you only have one mother, and while she did

what she did, one day she will be gone."

My father was always a peacemaker it seemed, and often offered the psychological effects of actions. He rarely spoke ill of my mother, even when I was the most frustrated with her. He never put her down, perhaps because he had his own indiscretions. Mostly he would say, "She has a disease and doesn't know any better."

"I don't want to call her."

"Okay."

And that is where it ended, at least for a while.

The next time I saw my mother and John was the summer of 1988, the year after I graduated high school. Lori, my girlfriend at the time, said she wanted to meet my mother. She and John were still living in High Point/Greensboro, but with no furniture factory.

It was a bizarre visit, to say the least. Lori and my mother went off to do some cross-stitching; I think Lori ended up cross-stitching some birds—geese—while we were there.

At one point, John cornered me outside and tried to talk to me—to apologize for all the things he had done. I told him to go to hell. "You knew what you were doing!! You son-of-a-bitch." It took all my willpower not to slug him, but I went back into the house and asked my brother if he wanted to go shopping.

Specifically, I wanted to take him shoe shopping. While we were growing up shoes were very special things for us. We often got hand-me-downs, or my mother would go buy them without us being with her. She often bought the wrong size but did not really seem to care. I recall one pair she bought: they were brown, with white stripes, and were several sizes too small so hurt my feet. I finally had to cut the toe section out of the front to even wear them. When she asked what happened I made up some story and she either believed it or did not care about it. Soon after I cut the toes out, Mrs. Hoppes, my friend's mother, noticed and had Scott give me an old pair of his that were my size.

So on this trip, I took Ralph to the Thom McAn store in the mall in Greensboro, because I got a discount. We bought several pairs of shoes.

The next time I would see my mother was after I had joined the Air Force, a few days before I left the country for the Incirlik Air Base in Turkey. I would arrive during the Desert Storm Conflict, but eventually, become part of Operation Provide Comfort through to the time I left in 1995, which would total a little over three and half years. My official job was a public affairs specialist, but I was also a journalist and editor for a weekly paper.

Before I was to embark on this journey, though, one of John's nephews committed suicide, so I went to his funeral. The funeral was, of course, a somber event, which was only compounded by all the young people there to see Alan.

I remember Alan from a few weeks I had spent with his family in Virginia Beach at the end of my eighth grade year. I remember talking to my brother about why Alan might have committed suicide and he speculated that John was molesting him; that Alan could not tell anyone and it was his way out of it.

I talked to my mother a few times while I was in Turkey. One time I called and found out that she had developed peripheral neuropathy, a painful, debilitating nerve disorder. John had told my mother he had called and informed me of her condition, but that I would not talk with her. It was a lie. I was so furious.

Not knowing anything about the disorder, I asked an Air Force doctor about it and her first question was if my mother drank.

I replied, "Heavily."

She told me that the alcohol was most likely the cause. I confronted my mother about what the doctor had said, but she denied my allegations. I am not sure why I expected anything else. She was paralyzed from the waist down for more than a year, but could not bring herself to say it was due to the alcohol. She would choose to drink over walking. Addictions are baffling.

Maureen Melia

The summer I had moved out on my own, Maureen Melia, a blue-eyed brunette, started working at the Thom McAn shoe store I was working at. I would quickly become an assistant manager, and we worked together for about a year.

She was very friendly and we got along really well. I gave her a raise, her first one.

Eventually, I moved to another store as an assistant manager, but Maureen and I remained friends. Over the course of the next three years, Lori and I would end our relationship a few times. I would date a few other people, but then Maureen began to hang out with Michelle, one of the new assistant managers at the store I was working at, so we would see each other quite regularly. We would often go over to party at Michelle's house, and stay late into the evening. At first, Maureen was dating someone and would bring him along, but finally, when they broke up, I decided to ask her out.

Maureen was hesitant, but agreed to go for dinner at the Olive Garden and to a movie with me. We went to Greenbrier Mall in Chesapeake, VA, and I bought John Lennon's Imagine CD at Mother's Record Store. We dated for a while and began hanging out with some of Maureen's friends from high school.

Things were going really well, but I was feeling like I was in a dead-end job. After I went to see the Air Force recruiter and was convinced I wanted to join, Maureen and I decided to get married. It was an informal proposal; we went to buy rings and told her parents. Everyone was happy, and so a wedding date was set for December 28, 1992. It was the same date as my grandparents' anniversary. But then the recruiter told me I should get married before I officially enlisted, as the Air Force could decide to send me to a place where wives could not go. We eloped on May 10, 1992, without telling anyone.

Maureen moved into my father's home as one of her sisters had moved into her parents' already cramped house. When I arrived at boot camp, I began sending pictures of myself home. Allison, my father's third wife, started taking the pictures to work and showing people. One of the ladies looked at a picture and quickly asked when I had gotten married. Allison said I had not yet but that I was engaged and the wedding was being planned. The lady got a magnifying glass out and showed Allison, as plain as day, the wedding band on my finger.

I called home that afternoon and the first question my father asked me was, "Are you married?"

"Yes."

"Well, congratulations!"

I called Maureen at work and left her a message that they knew.

My dad and Allison had a cake waiting for her when she arrived home that evening.

And then on December 28th, 1992, we had a beautiful ceremony at Ascension Catholic Church in Virginia Beach.

My mother was not invited.

U.S. Air Force

As I mentioned, I was enlisted in the U.S. Air Force from 1991-1995. I went to basic training in Texas and then went to journalism school at Fort Benjamin in Harrison, Indiana. I remember there was a lieutenant that came in on one of our last days of basic training. We had not seen many officers while at basic, so were all quite surprised by his visit.

I remember like it was yesterday. He met with us in the evening and read a quote that to this day has stuck with me. He said, "I want to read you a quote by John Stuart Mills, and I hope you will remember this as you carry out your service." And then he read:

"War is an ugly thing, but not the ugliest of things: the decayed and degraded state of moral and patriotic feeling which thinks that nothing is worth a war is much worse. When a people are used as mere human instruments for firing cannon or thrusting bayonets, in the service and for the selfish purposes of a master, such war degrades a people. A war to protect other human beings against tyrannical injustice; a war to give victory to their own ideas of right and good, and which is their own war, carried on for an honest purpose by their free choice— is often the means of their regeneration. A man who has nothing which he is willing to fight for, nothing which he cares more about than he does about his personal safety, is a miserable creature who has no chance of being free unless made and kept so by the exertions of better men than himself. As long as justice and injustice have not terminated their ever-renewing fight for ascendancy in the affairs of mankind, human beings must be willing, when a need is, to do battle for the one against the other."

As hard as I thought basic training was, this quote put things into perspective for me. On my first day at Ft. Benjamin, I reported in and was given my orders for my next assignment – Incirlik Air Base, Turkey. I had to go to the library and get an atlas out to see exactly where I was going. Journalism school was an exciting time for me. Not only was I was trained how to write, but also how to be a photojournalist; I even got to develop black and white film. It was a wonderful time for me, as I had always loved writing and photography.

A few months later, in March 1992, we arrived in Turkey. The ground war in Iraq was over, but we were in what was considered a hazardous duty zone and were participating in an active operation—Operation Provide Comfort. The objective of the operation was to defend Kurds fleeing their homes in Northern Iraq in the aftermath of the Gulf War and deliver humanitarian aid to them.

My first job upon arrival was as a staff writer for the base weekly paper. My job changed a few times while I was in Turkey—from staff writer to editor, and then to special projects. I met a number of people that I still have contact with to this day.

I was fortunate to see more than fifteen different countries and saw both good and bad in each of them. I think the Air Force was where I really started to focus on my leadership skills. It helped me forge my beliefs on how to lead.

While the military can be a very top-down leadership model, I saw, and experienced, a teamwork approach in my office and with the wing commanders I worked for while in Turkey. I worked for an NCOIC (Non-Commissioned Officer in Charge) Eddie Boykin who taught me that it was okay to be compassionate and be a boss. Eddie was a kind soul who loved everyone. He led with a servant leadership attitude and appreciated everyone's input.

The first officer I worked for was Captain Jerome Reed, who was from Farmville, Va. We used to smoke Marlboro Lights together and play basketball in the evening when we had time. The second officer, Captain Grant Sattler, who happened to be a great writer, was able to lead us through some very busy times at Incirlik. Second Lieutenant Pat Ryder (now Colonel) came to Turkey in the last year of my enlistment and taught me to have a growth mindset, to stay firm in my beliefs as a leader, and about the importance of kindness. All these men helped me grow to become a better man, a better writer, and a better military man.

The last 39th Wing Commander I worked under was Colonel John Berry, who retired as a Lieutenant General. John always liked me, mainly because I did not mind working hard. Often on the weekends, he would simply call my house and say, "Bill, I am going to work."

That was my cue to show up myself. Sometimes I would just sit in the Public Affairs Office all day and we would talk through certain things or if there were a special event or happening, I would take a picture. In 1994, he called me to his office and told me to have my Class A's ready as I would be accompanying him to meet the President of Turkey. I was so grateful for the opportunity. That evening we flew up to Istanbul and went to the Bosporus Palace Hotel. While we waited for President Abdullah Gül to arrive, John complimented me on the work I had been doing and told me he appreciated my work ethic. It was an exciting time in my life, and while I do not think I was appreciative for the experiences as they happened, I am grateful having served under these fine men, and the lessons I learned are still with me to this day.

I am proud to call myself a veteran and to have been a part of something bigger than myself.

My Mother Finally Leaves John

A few years later, I was back stateside and embarking on my new career as a teacher. I was staying with my in-laws in Virginia Beach while doing my undergraduate work at Old Dominion University; my wife lived four and half hours away in Sterling, VA, working on an associate's degree in Veterinary Technology.

It was around 1996 when my brother called me out of the blue. "Mom wants to leave John."

"Hell, it's about time!"

"Yes!"

Apparently, my mother had called my brother and her father to say she was leaving John because he had told her he wanted to be gay again.

I scoffed. "When did he stop?"

I called John, to let him know, that is to warn him, that I was on my way, "I'm not a little boy anymore and I am not afraid. I dare you to be there."

John was drunk and had a mouthful to say on the phone, but when Ralph, a family friend and I went to pack up my mother's stuff, he was nowhere to be found. He was a coward. He was a coward for molesting and taking advantage of young boys, and he was a coward when challenged by a man.

It had been about six years since I had seen my mother; even when I returned from the military, I did not go visit her. In fact, Old Dominion was in Norfolk, where she lived, and so I drove there every day, but still did not go see her. I simply needed to stay away.

When I walked into their house, it reminded me of how I grew up. The smell was the same. It was unclean and cluttered. The stale smell of alcohol permeated the air, and I remember stopping in the doorway as my memory caught up with me. I passed right by her. I did not even recognize her. She had aged so much and the alcohol had done so much to damage her body, I thought she was John's mother. She was not the woman I pictured from my childhood. Once a beautiful tan beached girl, she had become an old lady. I know part of this is time, but you could tell she had been living a hard life.

My half-sister, Leigh Anne, was there and she began to yell at me. "You have caused this!"

"I've caused what?"

"You have caused Mom to drink! You have made Mom this way because you left!"

"Leigh Anne, you have no idea what you are talking about. She has been like this for years! This did not happen overnight! In fact, I would say her drinking was one of the reasons I left!

Leigh Anne stormed upstairs. I was blown away by her comments. The fact that she was trying to put my mother's drinking all on me was absolutely preposterous.

Nothing was packed in the house, so we began throwing things into the back of the U-Haul. The place was cluttered and messy, which was no surprise. I had taken a few hundred dollars out of the cash machine on the way and gave it to my mother. She got in the U-Haul and drove back to North Carolina to live with her parents, at least for a short period of time. Ralph helped her get set up in a trailer on the same piece of property she lived in years ago, and her father bought her a car.

I did not see my mother again for about three years when my first child was born in 1999.

Becoming a Father

My first year teaching was also when I found out I would be a father. I was so excited. I wanted a girl first; I am not sure why. Maybe I thought I could not raise a boy because I was so broken. Either way, my daughter Emma came on June 23, 1999. She came early, and in the early morning. My wife woke me up and within minutes we were in the car. Of course, every light between our house and the hospital was red. My blood pressure still rises when I think about it.

Emma was born on my best friend's mother's birthday, and she was the first person I called. My brother drove up from North Carolina to see her and my father's mother came down from Pennsylvania. My father and his wife came out, too. And as soon as the doctor said it was okay, we took my sweet little baby girl down to North Carolina to see my grandparents and my mother.

I used to take Emma everywhere with me. I was always fearful that if I left her alone too long something bad would happen. I would wake her up just to hold her if I was late coming home—that was not very popular. I had this fascination with Paddington Bear with her and probably bought her way too many.

Emma has grown up to be a beautiful young woman. She is intelligent, loves music, and like her father, has a low tolerance for ignorant people.

It is not always perfect between us, as it is hard for me to understand the mind of an 18 year-old girl. I have yelled more than I would like to admit. Still, I am her biggest fan. I bought her a set of diamond studs for her sixteenth birthday. She traveled to Europe that same year, as I wanted her to know, as soon as possible, that the world was bigger than she was, but that she could still conquer it. I have raised her to be brave, and strong, and that she could do anything if she put the time in.

I tell her all the time, "You are what you say you are!"

daughter

tomorrow touches you too soon
while I smile for today
i hope yesterday I did my job
your hair falls gently across your face
time has stolen the little girl pigtails
you still smile when you see me
your soul is pure with ambition
your heart with journey
your spirit with song
the lilt in your laughter
the world is funny and complicated
tomorrow comes without notice
too many days are wished away
and I live for your tomorrow
the most precious of all
wishing I could slow down time
intelligent and faithful
God has plans for you
I love you - your Dad

My first son, Mitchell Thomas, came three years after Emma. He was supposed to be born on November 5, my best friend's birthday, and his namesake, but the doctor was delayed because he was stuck in a snowstorm returning from a conference. Maureen was so upset because she was afraid that the doctor she had been seeing all through her pregnancy would not be the one to deliver Mitchell. Everything, of course, would work out fine, and Mitchell came on November 7, Maureen's older twin sister's birthday.

He was a beautiful baby and looked just like my father. Unfortunately, his birth caused a six-month rife between my father and me.

My father and my best friend Jeff had a falling out years ago when Jeff called into question my father's behavior toward me. When I told my father what I was going to name my son, it did not go over well.

I first wanted to name Mitchell "Sebastian" after the first Sroufe who came to America from Germany, but that was vetoed by Maureen. Then, I thought perhaps we could give him a good German name like Wolfgang, but that was vetoed, too. Mitchell was introduced into the conversation and it sat well with me. His middle name, Thomas, is for Jeff's father who died in a naval airplane crash.

My father wanted me to name him William David Sroufe Jr. I did not even entertain naming him after me, and my father was furious over it, spouting, "I guess I don't have a son."

I was devastated by his words, and could not, and still do not, understand his behavior. He did not see Mitchell for six months when he finally called to apologize. Looking back, I think this was the first of many slips from sobriety for my dad.

Mitchell is an intelligent child. He almost spoke in complete sentences at 18 months old. There was a long period of time when we thought he was on the autism spectrum. He had some of the classic characteristics. He was very intelligent, was speaking full sentences as a young toddler, had an aversion to noises and textures, and would sometimes scream or make weird noises. He saw a specialist and was tested, but they said he was fine. He has grown out of most of the characteristics, now, and I have realized it is just who he is.

Mitchell has caused me more lack of sleep than the other two combined, though. I have learned how to be a better father because of him, as Mitchell requires patience; he tries mine almost every day. He is a gentle boy who loves cats, trains and Star Wars, which is interesting as Maureen and I were out watching Star Wars the night she went into labor. He loves the marching band and camping with the Boy Scouts. He is also a picky eater.

On Easter Sunday a few years ago, I was planting flowers in the front of the house and Mitchell was riding his scooter on the road. I had my earbuds in, but I heard a car screech and a thump. I looked down the road and Mitchell had been hit.

"I am okay!" He shouted back. "No, I'm not."

I swear it took ten years off my life. I nearly pulled the guy out of the car to beat him, but I went to Mitchell first and saw that his leg was obviously broken, so called 911 instead.

Emma was home and rode in the ambulance with him so I could drive. Maureen was at the store and met us there. The break was clean but required a cast. I slept by his side for the three nights he stayed in the hospital.

Benjamin came three years after Mitchell—a beautiful baby with blue eyes and red hair. Now I had a brunette, a blonde and a redheaded kid. I used to call them the Cosmopolitan Gang!

Benjamin is a funny kid and is kind to everyone he meets. It is tough being the baby, but he has managed it well. He is the favorite grandchild, as he loves to go with his Papa to do anything. He bowls, golfs, plays lacrosse as well as football, baseball, and basketball. He is also in middle school band.

We call him Wolfie as the same names I wanted for Mitchell

came into the conversation, but I had no luck this time either. He loves to go out to eat and is simply the slowest eater I have ever met. Like most brothers, he and Mitchell argue and I consistently talk to them about getting along. They do play Hot Wheels and Legos together.

sons
trees are climbed
upon the hill, tonka trucks have tumbled down
cars upon the furniture
zoomed to the end
hot wheels under feet
trains to no end
before you were born - I loved you
boys to become men
lessons to learn
about what is right
honor, patriotism, love, and life
honesty at all times
dignity at every turn
lessons I hope you have learned
ones I have shown you
faith above all
I love you – your Dad

Being a father has been the most rewarding experience I have encountered in my life. I am not perfect, and some things I should do I do not. There was a time when I spanked my children. I guess because I was spanked as a child. But one time while we were in New York visiting my cousin once, I remember Mitchell had done something I deemed wrong, so I was spanking him. I realized it was not working, but more importantly, I did not like how I felt. Something came over me and I became angry with myself for ever having spanked any of them. I never spanked them again.

I truly try to appreciate this time I have with them. As I work on this chapter, I am reflecting on the things we do as parents. For example, this past weekend was a busy one in my household. Mitchell plays the mellophone in the marching band and on Friday night I went to the football game to watch his performance and then take my youngest home. Saturday, my wife and I went to a portion of the competition to support him. Then yesterday morning, I got up at 6 AM to take Mitchell to an event in which the band was playing in support of the Hokie Half marathon. By noon, I was on the road driving to Richmond because I had to be there for a meeting early Monday morning.

I can tell you when I was growing up THAT never happened for me.

While I lived with my mother if I wanted to go to something I had to walk or ride my bike because my mother wouldn't take me and I didn't want to get in the car with John. When I lived with my father he would take me if he was not working, but I used public transportation or walked before I could drive. Hell, I remember when I got my driver's license my father was too busy to take me, so he just let me drive myself to the DMV, and I took the test and drove home.

I do not go to every event, of course, but I try. I had lunch with them at their elementary schools. I took my boy's hunting, flying, and rode with them on roller coasters. We have been to Disney, Busch Gardens, and Kings Dominion.

I will teach them how to drive, and how to work on their cars. I teach them how to cook and clean up. I will teach them how to plant and grow vegetables. I try and model hard work and resilience.

I continue to have my faults, of course. I think I yell too much when I should listen more. I give in too much when I should hold firm. I am sure there other things I do wrong, but I have tried to be the best father I could be, and I think they know I will always be in their corner.

And most importantly, that I love them unconditionally.

Being an educator and having kids go to school is a challenge. My kids, for the most part, have had great teachers and good experiences. A good friend of mine was their elementary principal, so I was lucky. In fact, to this day, my kids still hold Mr. Brian Kitts in high regard. He is a wonderful educator, and I still seek his advice. It has been rare that I have had a problem with one of my own kid's teacher. I have tried, particularly in my current position as superintendent, to not intervene unless I truly believed something was way out of line.

When Mitchell was in kindergarten, his teacher would call and tell us that Mitchell kept getting in everyone's personal space. I never taught below the eighth grade, but I thought to myself, *Isn't that what 6-year-olds do?*

Also, a teacher Emma had for science insisted on giving crosswords for assessments. Emma had the hardest time with them, and I thought they were a waste of time.

Mitchell has been the only one suspended from school. He earned most of the punishments he has gotten, and the only time I had an issue with a suspension was when the elementary band director decided on the day of the performance to send Mitchell home and not let him participate. There was no discussion and no one reached out to me to explain what had happened—only that he was not able to perform in the Winter

Holiday Performance.

I do not know that they have had a Mrs. Bailey in their public education career, but I am grateful for all of their teachers.

Professionally, I am proud of what I have accomplished so far - I finished my doctorate, wrote two poetry books and have become a school superintendent, but the thing I am most proud of is being a father. I have raised three beautiful children. I have given them all I could, sometimes too much, and sometimes not enough. They have had opportunities I never dreamed possible. My goal for them was always for them to be happy and productive citizens. I want them to work hard and appreciate the life they have enjoyed.

My Father's Passing

The first couple of years I lived with my father in Norfolk I went to many AA meetings with him. They were held at the Lutheran Church; I remember there was a lot of coffee and even more cigarette smoke. I would just sit there as they would go around the circle with each member introducing themselves.

"Hello, my name is Ralph, and I am an alcoholic."

It is a humbling experience to see broken people trying to heal themselves.

A disease has no preference—poor or rich, black or white, male or female. These people were trying to survive. I remember feeling that about my father—that he was simply surviving.

My father really worked his program and was sober for more than 20 years, before he was not.

My father was bright, but his demons kept him from being brilliant. He smoked a lot, and I think he lied more than I would like to admit. He loved me unconditionally, though his self-preservation came first. Demons can run deep in some people, and my father was no different. I think he thought he was smart enough to tackle his. My father's specialty as a psychologist was chemical dependency. When he was in private practice, he made his living helping other people conquer their drug and alcohol addictions . But as they say, it is always easier to help others heal than to deal with your own pain.

Relationships continued to be a struggle for my father as well. He and his third wife divorced and he soon married another. Even after we reconciled after Mitchell's birth, my father remained disconnected from me on some level. He was the Regional Manager in the Office of Licensing for the Virginia Department of Mental Health, Mental Retardation, and Substance

Abuse Services. To open a mental health facility in Virginia, you had to go through my father, so he had to travel throughout the state. He would sometimes come to Roanoke, which was only 30 miles from where I was living, but not come to see me or even let me know he was in town.

Somebody recently asked me why my brother did not come live with my father and me when I ran away all those years ago since he was also being abused. I think it was one of my father's greatest regrets that he did not. Remember, I was the one who made the first move and I am not sure if my father even though he had a choice. I was also at the age that I could legally make the decision where I wanted to live, but my brother was only ten. I loved my father, but deep down I do not know if he could have handled two kids anyways. Ralph was also so young when my father and mother divorced, that he did not really know him. What my father did for me was such a huge leap from his experiences with his own father, but doing it for both, or all three of us, just wasn't in his wheelhouse.

On January 2, 2009, I got a phone call from Debra, my father's fourth wife.

"Bill, your father's had a stroke."

I forced myself to ask, "Is he…"

"We're rushing him to the hospital," she cried. "You have to come here.

Now."

I was not my father's benefactor but I was the name in his living will, so I grabbed the documents and got ready in about twenty minutes. My wife's parents rushed over to take care of our kids. I did not know if he was going to live or die, but I did not want to take my kids to what I thought was going to be complete chaos.

We were an hour into the drive when the pastor called me and told me that my father had died. And that it was suicide.

Time stopped.

I was driving, so I could not lose control.

"No!!!!!" I screamed out loud. "How could he do this?" I was crying, furiously crying.

I was in disbelief; it was like an out-of-body experience. I felt like I was a spirit watching myself trying not to lose control. Maureen just sat in silence as I berated his spirit.

"You selfish son of a bitch!"

I rebuked his death as cowardly. I was so mad at him I could not see straight. He always tried to raise me not to overreact, but that perhaps spurred my rage.

Finally, I calmed down because I knew I had to call a few people. I started with my brother. I allowed him to call our sister, but I called my aunt, uncle, and step-grandfather. My father's mother was still alive, but she had Alzheimer's and we decided not to tell her.

Everybody was as shocked as I was. I seriously had no clue that he was in that state of mind. In fact, I had called him the day before to wish him a Happy New Year, and he had not said anything was wrong.

I remember I was driving to the mall and it was just the same old conversation. I asked, "How are you?"

He replied, "I'm fine. Going grocery shopping."

"Okay, well I'll speak with you later. I love you."

"I love you, too," were the last words he would ever say to me.

There was no note. The story according to his wife was that they had been in an argument the night before. She did not say exactly what the fight was about, but my father had been drinking. He took off in his car with a bottle of wine, and she did not stop him.

Eventually, she went to bed. The next morning, she woke up and found my father sitting on his bed. He had been sleeping in the guest room as they had not been getting along. She had not heard him come home, so was not sure if he had slept or not.

She said he was lucid and just said, "I've done something. I have taken an entire bottle of blood pressure meds and drank a bottle of wine. I am feeling very anxious. Can you get me a Zanax?"

To this day, I do not understand why, but Debra got him the pills. She had not called for emergency assistance yet either, she said because he told her not to.

They were smoking a cigarette when it all hit my father and he began to show the signs of a stroke. Debra then called 911, but given the number of pills and amount of wine in him, there was no turning back.

I have never told my kids how he died.

When my wife's parents told our kids that my father had passed away, Mitchell, who was just a little guy at seven years old, was apparently really sad for me and said, "Now he won't have a daddy."

When I heard this, I almost got in the car and went to get them. It had only been a couple days, but I really needed them. I could not sleep. I did not sleep for almost 48 hours when he died.

It was all just so pointless.

Even after almost nine years, there is still a selfish part of me that is pissed off that he did it like this and never gave me a chance to say goodbye. That he has missed so many special moments, like when my daughter graduated. Now she is in college, and as a proud parent, I get to take credit for part of that. He, of all people, should have known that.

But I work to remember who he was when he was healthy. He loved his work.

He liked to laugh but had a dry sense of humor.

He loved Chinese food. Orange beef was his favorite dish and butter pecan his favorite ice cream.

He smoked Marlboro Lights—shorts. He used to iron his jeans.

I loved him beyond belief and hated him for taking his own life. Damn, I am still angry.

repealed

in the fog of time when will I return?
not ready for my birth and death must refrain
in the days before what could you have thought?
our conversation was short,
but our lives were not
in your final words
what am I to say to my children
who ask about your dying day
yesterday seems clear
upon your crown of thorns
the words of death surround the years and more
I seek to know
I know I never will
what could I have done?
how could I have healed?
a broken heart untold
today I pray alone for your soul repealed

Ralph Jr.

Since the time I left Ellenboro, I have struggled in my relationships with my siblings. In Dr. Ruby Payne's book *A Framework for Understanding Poverty*, she says that to escape poverty, and all the luggage that comes with it, you have to cut the relationships of the past. I think that is part of what I have done over the years. I have had to sever many relationships, and create strong boundaries in others.

Lisa got married at just sixteen years old, and many times after. She was a heavy drug user, and it was uncomfortable for me to even be around that part of my family. Ralph and I had begun to rebuild our relationship after my daughter was born. We saw each other periodically at first, and then more regularly over the years, and we talked all of the time. We had even taken some short vacations together and had made plans to move closer to one another. But then on June 14, 2009, just six months after my father had committed suicide, Ralph also passed away.

I had spoken with him a few times that day, as it was a tumultuous time in his life. He was separating from his second wife and was in the process of moving things out of his house. The last time we talked, he was driving on the highway. We made some jokes, as usual, but then he told me he was not feeling well. He was driving a truck and towing a trailer he was unfamiliar with, so was going to pull over.

I told him, "You must be anxious with everything going on. Just rest and give me a call later."

He never called me back. It was a Saturday and I called him a few times over the weekend, but nothing. I went to work on Monday and left my cell phone in my office while speaking with the custodians in the building. I returned to find a missed call from an unknown number. Thinking Ralph had dropped his phone in the lake or something, I called the number back.

I got a North Carolina State Trooper. He explained that my brother was dead.

Ralph's truck had stayed parked on the side of the road all weekend, but finally Monday morning someone looked inside and discovered his body. He had had a massive heart attack.

I was the last person he spoke with.

To say I was devastated would be an understatement. Even to this day, I would never wish that amount of grief on my worst enemies. In retrospect, I think my dad and brother's deaths impacted me more than any of the other things combined.

I am not sure if it would have mattered if they died years apart, but because their deaths were only in a six-month span, I never had a chance to deal with one blow before the other came. Especially, with my father's death being a suicide. Suicide always has its own level of questions, of what ifs. And then my brother. He was just 36 years old.

My family and I were scheduled to go to Disney World to celebrate my daughter's tenth birthday. My brother's funeral was scheduled right before our vacation, so we first made our way to Ellenboro for the funeral.

As we stood in line to greet people, person after person came through offering their sympathy and I would ask who they were if I did not know. Because I had left the town when I was fifteen, I actually did not recognize many people there. Most people knew who I was, though, because my brother and I looked a lot alike.

My grandfather had been gone for a few years, having passed away in 2004. He had had a stroke a year before his death and I flew down to Tampa Bay where he had moved to visit him. His mind was unstable and he thought he had night-time duty on a ship. I played along, as to not add to his confusion. There had been some turmoil between my mother and her sister as well. My mother was the oldest, but the fight came down to money. The only good thing that came out of my grandfather's death was that my cousin Nicole and I became close again.

She is my first cousin and lives in Warwick, NY. Sometimes I feel she is the only family I have outside of my house. I am most grateful to her, and she may never know how important she is to me.

So this left Ellenboro mostly filled with strange faces. I did recognize two people though: one was my Great Aunt Margaret, and the other was my sixth grade teacher Mrs. Frances Bailey.

I hugged her and cried.

I had never forgotten this woman, and she proved to me once again how important I was to her.

Moving Forward with my Mother

To this day people give me a hard time because I do not have a connection with my mother. The place where I work is small, so colleagues always ask me, "How come you don't call your mom?"

The reason? Because it is not a natural thing; and I feel no connection to her.

How could I?

She let a predator into our lives, into our beds. She did not protect us. No one protected us. This became especially hard to understand when I had children of my own. Our kids are our most precious gifts, and I feel so protective of them all of the time. I am especially guarded about them coming anywhere close to that world, even though it is just a memory. People often say that normal is not clearly defined, but I can say I have tried to ensure my children grow up in a normal life, or at least my version of it. The truth is I learned many things growing up like I did—*particularly things not to do.*

In all fairness when my mother has been around my children, everything has been fine, but I do not want my kids exposed to the chaotic memories of my childhood.

Sometimes I do call her out of guilt. She loves Facebook messenger, so I can communicate without having to speak to her. It is just kind of agonizing to speak to her. My mother is a negative person. She is bitter. She thinks she knows who I am. And that is okay.

I did see her recently when my brother's daughter got married in North Carolina. My niece wanted me to come so I went with my daughter. I really did not want to go, as it is still really hard to go back there. Even though it has been 35 years, it still makes me very uncomfortable.

That part of North Carolina, Cleveland, and Rutherfordton County was just destroyed economically after NAFTA. Everybody who lived there made a living in some kind of mill. Nobody was getting rich, but everybody was working and providing for their families. It was really sad to see. The mills are all shut down. There are just empty halls now.

I thought about how different my life would be if I had not had the courage that day to run away. I probably would have ended up getting a job at one of the mills, getting married right out of high school and having a dozen kids.

My kids do not really know what my childhood was like. They have lived in the same place their entire lives. Our electricity has never been turned off.

Police have not knocked on our door… You know, the simple things.

My daughter had gone back with me a couple years before as well when Mrs. Freeman, my former math teacher, and friend Jack's mother, had passed away. Jack called me and asked if I could write a poem for his mom, then come down to the funeral and read it. I said sure, wrote one and sent it to him. He thought it was perfect and so put it in the memorial booklet.

I drove down to the funeral, read it and left. And that was it—in about four hours.

This time, though, I set up a lunch with my 90 year-old great aunt. My grandfather had two siblings and everybody had passed away except for her.

And, of course, while I was in for the wedding, I saw my mother. It had been a number of years since I had seen her. When I see her now it is not like when I used to see her; I can be more dismissive of her. I am not trying to be mean, but I cannot do the "crazy," so I just walk away.

It is also difficult because she looks back and makes up stories of "spoiled" childhoods that never happened. She tries to give me parenting advice as if she did the things she is suggesting. For instance, she may tell me to pay for my daughter's college tuition or buy her a car, even though she did neither, not even close.

John's Death

After John and my mother broke up, John went back to Danny—Uncle Danny. I am not sure how my mother felt about that. I never asked. When we had first moved to Austin, Danny lived with us, but then at some point, I do not remember when he left. Looking back, I have wondered not only why my mother married John, but why John, an openly gay man with a partner, married my mother. I should clarify. Uncle Danny never touched us; he loved us. To be honest, I think Danny was in and out of the picture for years and years and years.

Danny died in the middle of the night apparently from some adverse reaction to a medication.

Then, approximately five years ago, John died of cirrhosis.

It is an odd ending to a tragic story. Out of the blue, my mother called me and told me he had died. They had been separated for years but never divorced and she talked as if I cared that he was gone. I only cared because out of all the people on Earth, he is the only person I would have killed myself. The truth is I would have put a bullet in him given the chance.

I hated him.

I hated the sound of his name.

I hated what he had done to my brother and me.

I hated I had been ashamed of something he did for decades.

I hated what he had robbed from me.

I hated that he robbed something from my mother.

But then after years of it, I realized I could not carry that hate anymore. I would never forgive him, but he was gone. I was safe. It is no more to me than a moment in history. In the end, he was no more than a person I would have passed on the street without a second thought.

That is where I need it to be, so I can move forward.

ng, Bill, I ...
experience as the m...
and rewarding honor of...
anks for remembering and
eng me in this way!
With deepest love and respect,
Frances Bailey

Mrs. Frances Bailey and me at Patrick County High School.

These are the glasses Mrs. Bailey made sure I got.

1st Report Period *Bill is a good student and has the potential to be an A student. His talking is improving.*

2nd Report Period

3rd Report Period

4th Report Period

PARENT'S SIGNATURE

1. *Mr. John D. Kilgore*

2.

3. *Mrs. ___ Kilgore*

4.

NORTH CAROLINA PUBLIC SCHOOLS
RUTHERFORD COUNTY SCHOOLS

PROGRESS REPORT
GRADES 4-8

_____ *Ellenboro* _____ School

Pupil's Name *Bill Kilgore* Grade *6*

School Year *80-'81* Teacher *S. Smith*

SCHOOL SUPERINTENDENT'S MESSAGE

Dear Parents:
This report represents the conscientious effort of the teachers in judging the progress of your child.

We invite you to visit the school and talk with the teacher about the progress of your child and also about the educational help you could give the child at home. Educational progress to a large extent is dependent on the cooperation that exists between parents and teachers.

DR. DOUGLAS L. PEARSON
Superintendent

ATTENDANCE	Report Period		
	1	2	3
Days Attended	44	44	42
Days Absent	1		3
Days Tardy			

RECORD OF PROMOTION		
Date	Promoted or Retained	G
6/8/81	*Promoted*	7

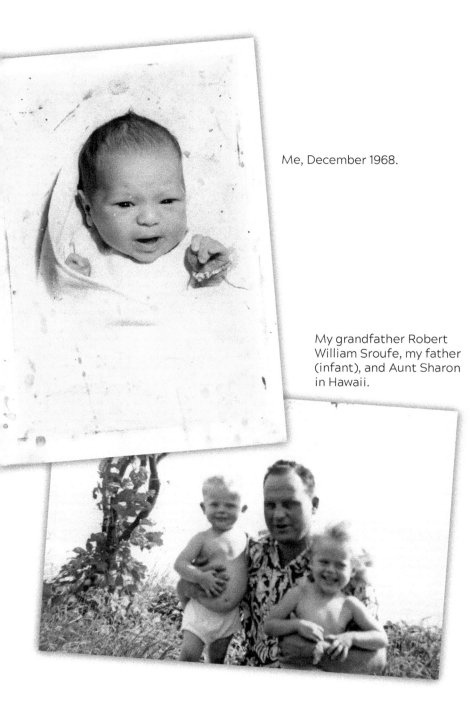

Me, December 1968.

My grandfather Robert William Sroufe, my father (infant), and Aunt Sharon in Hawaii.

ELLENBORO ELEM. 79   MISS KING   2 & 3 RD. GRADE

MR. WAYNE S. YORK
Principal

ELLENBORO ELEMENTARY SCHOOL
Ellenboro, North Carolina
1979-80

MISS HELEN WILLIAMSON
Grade 5

My grandmother
Sarah D. Greene.

My grandfather
William E.
Greene,
mother Karen
Kilgore, and
grandmother
Sara D. Greene.

My great grandparents J. Gillard and Adelaide B. Greene.

William E. Greene, my grandfather

My father Ralph Sroufe, Sr. in Basic Training.

My mother.

My mother and father at my mother's prom.

Lisa Karen, Ralph Edwin Jr., and William David in 1976 in Austin, TX.

My mother Karen, little brother Ralph, father, me, and Lisa at my Aunt Marilyn's wedding.

Me on the beach at a local park

My father Ralph E. Sroufe.

My favorite picture of my father, close to the end of his life.

My baseball team.

Ralph Edwin.

Defense Information School 1991 in Indianapolis, IN.

The first photo taken of me when I went to live with my father.

The day I met Leland Melvin.

Maureen and I at the December 1990 Semiformal 2TA.

My children (left to right) Benjamin, Mitchell and Emma

PART II

Teaching

In 1994, I came home on leave from the Air Force and my very good friend, Andrea Tottossy, who was a teacher and would later become my children's godmother, invited me to come along on a field trip with her as an extra chaperone. We went on a haunted trail, as it was around Halloween.

I thought to myself, *I kind of like this.*

So, just like that, I decided to embark on one of the most fulfilling careers I could have ever imagined. At that moment, I decided to get out of the military, setting my sights on becoming a teacher.

I returned from Turkey in April of 1995 after having served four years in the US Air Force. I had been accepted to Old Dominion University, and promptly met with the counselors to lay out the path to an education degree. As I have said, I worked a number of different jobs while going to school, including writing for the *Virginian Pilot*, writing restaurant reviews, and with desktop publishing at Kinkos.

During my preparations to become a teacher, I did a Practicum teaching seventh grade civics at Azalea Garden Middle School in Norfolk, VA. The school had a lot of diversity particularly given its location. I inquired about it once and my practicum teacher told me they bussed kids in from the housing projects. Even considering my background, I had never encountered a situation like this. I remember one girl who was about 12 years old came to school with her pajamas on, including pink fuzzy slippers. Her mom, who was a prostitute, had sent her out of the house for the night and the girl had to sleep under a bridge. But she still came to school.

I was shocked and overwhelmed. I remember thinking that I wanted to help make a difference to kids like this; I wanted to be an ear for them to talk with, and to help however I could.

I graduated with a BS in Interdisciplinary Studies and an MS Ed in 1998.

The Wednesday before graduation, I attended a teacher's job fair. My wife and I had decided to move to the western part of Virginia to escape the crowding and traffic of the Hampton Roads area. I did a "pre" interview with the human resource officer from Roanoke County, and he invited me to come to Roanoke the following Monday.

I arrived on Sunday to explore the area, before being interviewed by two principals on a Monday morning. I went home with no job offer, but a few days later Mr. Wood, the principal of Northside Middle School, called me and offered me a job teaching eighth grade physical science and world geography at Northside Middle School. He also told me I would be doing the yearbook and coaching girls' volleyball. I was delighted to be employed.

The entire first year I taught, I just walked around the halls in disbelief. I remember thinking, *I can't believe someone is actually paying me to do this!*

Having come from a career in the military, this was beyond a wonderful experience. I tried at every turn to push the envelope with my students, though. I tried to build relationships with them, and their families.

Realizing, how much energy teaching takes, physically, mentally and emotionally, shortly after I began I wrote many of my former teachers and apologized for my behavior during my tenure in their classroom. I only received one letter back, and that was from Mrs. Bailey. She said she remembered me.

Even though I was enjoying myself immensely, I briefly left teaching after two years, as I got offered a job as a yearbook salesman. It paid about $18,000 more than I was making, and with a new baby, we needed the money. I met a tremendous amount of people, but never liked the sales part of the job, so within a year I was back in the classroom.

I got a job teaching information technology, graphic design and animation classes at a charter school in Roanoke City at Blue Ridge Technical Academy. It was a high school ahead of its time, so never really got off the ground. The concept was to allow students who might not fit the mold of your typical high school student, for varying reasons, to explore their interests in the workforce through internships, job shadowing, etc.

However, the best time I ever had in the classroom came from my last teaching position at Christiansburg Middle School, which was just three miles from my house. I taught eighth grade civics and finally felt like I was making an impact. I think I realized some of the things I had done in the past in terms of teaching were the wrong approach.

I worked for a principal named Lou Barlow. He had one leg shorter than the other, but would still park in the furthest spot in the parking lot. He was such a great leader. I remember him telling me to build relationships with kids—to not just call the parents when kids are in trouble, but for the good things, too. He told me to have high expectations, but only for things that counted. I did what he said.

The first thing I did was change the way I thought about homework. I used to count it against a student if they did not hand in an assignment, but then remembered how it was when I was growing up; how I may not have been able to complete something because of the lack of support, or even chaos, that was going on at home.

I started incorporating music and PowerPoint slides into my lessons and brought in guest speakers. I challenged my students to become active in their community and to hold their representatives accountable. I also changed how I spoke about my own subject. I would tell the students that civics was the most important class of the day; and that they would be fools to miss it.

I was trying my best to be a teacher that a student would look back on favorably, but I made mistakes, of course. I remember I had an autistic student in my room. He was high functioning, and I remember thinking that he could do the work, but just would not. I held him to the same standard as I did everyone else and he was failing my class.

At the end of the year, he scored a perfect 600 on his Standards of Learning test, though, and I realized what I had done was wrong. So I went back and changed his grade to an "A".

While I was teaching at Christiansburg Middle School I would do everything I could to give my students an advantage. While planning our Washington DC field trip, I solicited eBay sellers who had disposable cameras to get one for each student. I wanted everyone to have the opportunity to take pictures. Also, I remember at Christmas the eighth grade teachers (the other grades did similar things) took up money and solicited free items from stores to give to students we thought needed items. I led the SCA (Student Council Activity), which is an extra-curricular activity that meets once a month after school. Each History/Civics class selects a student council representative at the beginning of the year. The representative must be reliable, enthusiastic and energetic. They must be interested in helping our school and community, as well as be interested in learning about democracy and leadership. The student council representatives share ideas, interests, and concerns from the student body in a diplomatic forum.

They also help plan school-wide activities, community projects, and school initiatives. One year, we did a coat drive and took up a special Montgomery County Christmas Store collection. One of the parents even built me special collection boxes; it really brought us all together as a community.

I also tried to think of out-of-the-box ways of relating to students, even when we were in disagreement. For example, my second year at the middle school, I had a few students who did not want to stand for the Pledge of Allegiance, not due to some stand against the pledge, but rather out of laziness and being stubborn. I would often go to their desks and ask them to stand but told them they did not have to recite the pledge. I used this as a teachable moment, explaining to my students their rights to exercise their First Amendment right.

Still, it bothered me that the students would not stand, so I asked a WWII veteran to come by my classroom and tell the students about his experiences. I also played a recording of my grandfather telling his story about Pearl Harbor. I had heard the story a number of times as a kid, but when I was doing my undergraduate work, we had to interview a veteran. Of course, my grandfather was the first person who came to mind. I cherish the recording mostly because he is speaking to me directly, just as if I was there with him. It is a powerful testament to who he was as a person. The students never sat for the pledge again.

At the end of my first year at Christiansburg Middle School, on June 5, 2004, President Ronald Reagan died. I had such a great group of kids that year I decided I would take some students to Washington DC for the president's funeral. I asked Mr.

Barlow, the principal if there would be any issues with my plans. He gave me the go-ahead but advised me to take another adult with me.

I chose a few students whose parents I had built great relationships with and called them explaining my plans. They all thought it was an excellent idea, and the students were excited. Although they were not as excited about having to meet at the school at 4 AM to make the nearly five-hour drive.

The drive went smoothly, though. We parked in Ballston, VA, and took the Metro over. It was a hot June day and we stood in line for four or five hours. I have never experienced anything before or since like what we did that day. We baked in the sun but finally got our turn to walk around the casket in the center rotunda in the Capital Building. It was draped in the American flag. The kids were thrilled, and truth is told, so was I, because we each got a small card as a souvenir marking our attendance. It was cream with gold writing and the presidential seal.

Nearly fourteen years later, whenever I run into these students they tell me about that day, and about how important it was, and still is, to them.

As educators, the most rewarding thing is hearing about the impact we have made. A few of my students have kept in contact over the years. It has meant everything to me, so I thought I would share a few of these connections.

One student, Desiree, was admittedly one of my favorites. She had a love for Kenny Chesney and all things America. She recently sent me a note that reads:

My favorite thing about you was how you not only were a teacher that made learning fun, but you also took time to get to know your students as people, not just as someone who you saw for a few hours a day. You were not just a teacher that I saw every day but you and your class were my favorite part of the day. You are the reason I wanted to learn so much about our presidents and though you probably do not know it, you were part of the reason why I chose criminal justice as my major at Radford! Of all the teachers I have had, you were and have always been my favorite teacher! Not many teachers will mourn with you when your favorite person in the world marries someone other than you (lol)! You helped shape me into who I am in just a matter of a year and I am very thankful for that!

After seeing a post on social media one day, I asked another student, Ryan, why I was his favorite teacher. He said this: "To this day I still consider you one of the best teachers I've ever had. I walked into your eighth grade civics class without a single care regarding our government. You turned that around. Rather than using the traditional methods of simply giving your students notes and tests to take, you encouraged a lot of conversation to really engage us in politics. At the time I was in your class, campaigns had begun for the 2004 presidential election. This was a great opportunity for you to really get us involved with both formal debates and informal discussions regarding the views of all sides of the political spectrum. On top of your teaching methods, you also connected with your students on a personal level, which not only made the class informative but made you want to be there to learn about our government. I can honestly say that the reason I am so involved and tuned in to politics today is that of your class."

But the greatest compliment is when a student is inspired themselves to embark on this most fulfilling career, and so I would like to share one more student reflection: "What I enjoyed most about you as a teacher is a way you took an interest in us. You made connections with us and made us feel important. During your class, you treated us with respect. I also learned a lot from you and it had a big impact on my own teaching methods. I think I took a lot from the way you treated us and I treat my students that way as well. My eighth grade year inspired me to teach middle school!"

One of the bittersweet joys of teaching, though, is seeing students grow over the years. Even though I taught eighth grade, I have been invited and have attended many graduations. I have seen kids who started dating in my class get married and even welcome their first child.

I recently had a brief stay in the hospital. As I was lying there in bed, one of the nurses came in and said, "Why do I know you?"

I looked right at her and said, "I taught your daughter."

"Oh yeah, she's 28 now and has a kid," she replied.

Ugh. How did that happen?

To me, she should still be a teenager. I am glad that they remember me, though. That is what I always wanted. To have an impact—to have a *positive* impact—on kids' lives.

I have parents to this day who call me for support, too. Even though a child may now be 30 years old, the parents can still get upset because they are not doing what they want them to do. And so they call me. "Hey, can you go and see Chris? He'll listen to you."

The truth is if Mrs. Bailey called me right now and told me to do something I would be sort of hesitant to say no. I still want to please her. That is what I have always wanted to be—a Mrs. Bailey for some kid.

I have written letters of reference, hired former students, attended weddings, baptisms, and unfortunately, funerals.

Radford University

In 2006, I received my administrative endorsement from Radford University while I was still teaching at Christiansburg Middle School. The principal ended up giving me a master key and would pull me from class throughout the year to help cover administrative duties. I wrote Mrs. Bailey to update her on my current status and once again, she wrote me back.

She asked about my family and told me she was proud of who I had become. She told me she had confidence in me at a young age that I would grow up and do something good with my life. I do not know how the hell she could have, but those words, then and now, mean so much to me because I knew she meant it. Even after all these years, Mrs. Bailey never had to write me a single letter. She never had to take the time to worry about an annoying kid from 20 years before, but she did because that is who she is. She had a trait that is lost on some people. She knew the value of a relationship and the responsibility that teachers have to their students. It is one of the reasons that I most often tell former students when I see them, "Please let me know if I can do anything to help you."

I am proud to write letters of reference, attend weddings, and chat with them in the middle of the grocery store. In one letter I wrote to Mrs. Bailey, I apologized to her for my behavior, and when Mrs. Bailey wrote me back she said I was just a regular sixth grader. I wasn't, but to Mrs. Bailey I was. We came to her— some of us broken, battered and bruised— and she took us all into her classroom and held us to the highest standards because she knew the value of an education.

However we came to her through her classroom door, she was not going to let us leave without knowing she cared about us and cared about our education.

She will always have a legacy with me as the epitome of a teacher, and cornerstone of every school building in America. But still, there is only one Mrs. Bailey.

Meadows of Dan Elementary

In 2006, on the day before I started my fourth year teaching eighth grade civics at Christiansburg Middle School, I got a call from Mr. Walter Broom, the assistant superintendent in Patrick County, VA. He asked if I would be interested in interviewing for a principal position at Meadows of Dan Elementary. When I got the call, I was with some fellow teachers and one of them, Chris Wikstrom, was dating a girl from Patrick. That was my only knowledge of the place. The next day, my first day back at school, I left early and interviewed at the school board office with about 15 people. I felt good about the interview, and the next morning before my first class, Mr. Broom called me. "Bill?"

"Yes?"

"Walt Broom, here. Wondering if you would like to come and work for us in Patrick County."

"Of course, that would be great."

We talked about the logistics of my contract, and I tried to focus on what he was saying, but I could not stop thinking about how some 25 years after spending a weekend scrounging around a scummy trailer for 25 cents to pay Mr. York back for stealing an ice cream, *I* was going to be *the principal*. Meadows of Dan Elementary, which was built in 1937, is at an altitude of 2,847 feet, and only had a little over 130 kids PreK-7, but I was going to be its leader.

I realized quickly that it is a tough thing going right from the classroom to becoming the principal of a whole school. Everyone in the building had more experience in education than I did, but everyone also respected me as the principal.

Meadows of Dan Elementary is much like a small private school, which I loved. It is a close-knit community that cares

deeply about tradition and history. The students are very respect-
ful and I learned tremendous lessons about building relationships and dealing with parents in those first two years.

I was never a fan of suspending students. After all, our job
is to teach them, and that is difficult to do when they were at
home. So, sometimes I would call parents and report to them
what had happened with their child. I would ask if they could
handle it for me, or if I should suspend their child. The parents
would always guarantee me that it would not happen again, and
most often it did not. I gained a lot of respect from parents by
being fair and preferring to keep kids in school as much as possible. It did not always work, and sometimes students got suspended, but not very often.

As any teacher knows, the most difficult thing to deal with
is losing a student way too young. My second year at Meadows
of Dan, my son Mitchell attended PreK there. It was about a
35-minute ride from my house and we traveled Rt. 8, which is
a two-lane road. One morning, traffic was backed up and so we
detoured through a neighborhood in Riner, VA. I could see from
a distance that there had been a bad car accident and there were
a number of first responders on scene. Mitchell and I arrived at
the school, and shortly after I got a call from Crystal Smith, the
math teacher on my team at Christiansburg Middle School. She
told me that a former student of ours had been in a car accident
and was killed that morning.

"On Route 8?" I asked.

"Yes, how did you know?"

"I went by the accident this morning."

We were both horrified by the news, and after talking with
my other team members, three of the four of us went to her funeral. Her mother was so appreciative that we came. It was one

of the saddest days I have encountered as an educator.

I was at Meadows of Dan Elementary two years before transferring to Woolwine Elementary upon the request of the superintendent.

Woolwine Elementary

It was announced in April 2008, that I would be transferring to Woolwine Elementary. It was closer to my house, and I felt it was a great opportunity, as it had double the amount of teachers and about 250 kids PreK-7. I arrived July 1, 2008, but my then-secretary Mrs. Faye Brannon was on vacation, along with the custodial staff. I remember sitting in the office going through files, just trying to find things.

I was beginning to make my way as an administrator, though, and Woolwine Elementary School was very successful under my leadership. We were a Title I Distinguished School 5 years in a row, a Governors Excellence Award winner, and often had the highest percentage of perfect scores on SOL (Standards of Learning) Tests in the district. Woolwine Elementary was also a school that loved its traditions. We had a Veterans' Day ceremony, Halloween carnival, beauty pageants, and annual trips to Jamestown, Richmond, and Washington DC.

While at both schools, I looked for alternative fundraising ideas, as I hated the idea of my students peddling junk. I also did not think it was something a school with a 50% poverty level should engage in. Instead, we made apple butter, sold cookie dough, and hosted spaghetti dinners. If you have food, lots of people will always show up.

My best memories come from accompanying the students on overnight field trips to Jamestown, Richmond or Washington DC. I made arrangements for my students to meet Virginia US Senator Mark Warner, who was also a former Virginia Governor. We also rode in private subway cars to the capitol. The highlight for most of them would be the times we toured the White House.

I have always been in awe of teachers and the impact they have on students. At Woolwine Elementary, there is a teacher who has been teaching 40 plus years and is still always in it for the kids. She is an old school teacher who has high expectations, but in my five years as principal, I had more adults come back as former students to see Mrs. Linda Hopkins than any other teacher. They came from all walks of life, but one student's story, in particular, has stuck with me.

One day, a young man—a 3rd Infantry Regiment, "The Old Guard" soldier at the Tomb of the Unknown Soldier—came to see Mrs. Hopkins to thank her for being his teacher. He told her that his success was due to her high expectations. It was about a week or so before our trip to Washington DC and he invited our seventh graders to lay a wreath at the tomb, an honor reserved for dignitaries. I was astonished by his offer and so happy for our students to see not only the impact a teacher can have on a person, but also for the opportunity granted to them because of Mrs. Hopkins impact.

Having fostered so many relationships, when I was appointed the interim superintendent in 2014, I felt I had an advantage, especially when I would go to the high school. I knew so many of the students because of the time I had spent in the building. It has been a real joy to watch them grow up and become young men and women.

Division Superintendent

One of the proudest moments in my life as an educator was being named Division Superintendent of Patrick County Public Schools in May 2014 after having been the interim since February 2014. I went about my job as I have done everything my entire life—full throttle. I inherited a district that had four schools in school improvement and Patrick County was 75 out of 132 on Standards of Learning performance. I am not sure I quoted the movie directly, but when interviewing with the school board I took a quote from the Patrick Swayze movie *Road House*—"It'll get worse before it gets better."

They continued through their process, and I was offered the position.

The morning after I was approved as the new superintendent, I got into my car and my phone rang.

"Hello."

"Bill, this is Frances Bailey."

I felt like a little kid again, "Yes ma'am."

"Congratulations, I am very proud of you. Debbie (her daughter) called me last night and said you were officially appointed as the superintendent."

"Yes, ma'am."

"Well I won't keep you, but I just wanted you to know how proud I am of you."

"Thank you, Mrs. Bailey."

And that was it. A short phone call that meant the world to me. I was beaming that she called me.

When I hung up the phone, it really hit me how pivotal Mrs. Bailey was in my life. How that speech about courage in the sixth grade, in the dingy hallway of Ellenboro Elementary, changed my life.

Mrs. Bailey probably never even realized it. She always treated me like I was special, but the thing is, she did not treat me any different than she did any other student. It was not like I was the center of attention in her classroom. Every kid was the center of attention in her classroom.

As an educator, I have gotten things wrong more than once. The honest thing about teaching is that sometimes you like some kids more than others. Some make it hard for you to like them, but you do your best. I know looking back there were times that I could have done better by some of my students. I could have been less rigid, and looked past how they were acting, and tried to find out why. I did not always do that, even though I needed it myself as a child.

We are all human; we all make mistakes.

In my position now, as division superintendent, I am constantly asking people to be better. Our job is to do all we can and then get up and be better the next day.

I talk about impact. I talk about the good and bad of teaching but also remind people that you cannot recapture a day. You cannot get time back. I tell them that teaching is hard but worth it. I challenge them, as I do myself, to get up every day and be better.

Every student deserves that level of commitment.

Two years ago, I did the opening of our convocation for my school district. One of my points was that although we were one of the lowest funded districts in the Commonwealth, still, in the past couple of years at least, we performed very highly. I credited this to us building relationships with kids.

There were some hard personnel decisions and movements in the district that were necessary to make. I spent a lot of time at events, fostering relationships and building new ones. I was on the local radio station and getting the word out that my intention was to make Patrick County Public Schools the best in the Commonwealth and putting the education of the students first.

Over the course of the next three years, I would attend many conferences on education and leadership and read more than 200 books. In fact, in my short tenure, my team and I embarked to not only rejuvenate the Patrick County Public Schools instructional program, but to also revitalize classrooms, libraries, and technology. I addressed this by setting aside any predetermined mode of thinking about socioeconomic status, and simply imagining and engineering opportunities for students of Patrick County Public Schools.

The stability of the instructional program was my first order of business.

My team and I endeavored to establish Professional Learning Communities (PLCs) within schools to provide teachers with the opportunity to reflect on their instructional practice and consider the effect their instruction had on students and utilize the information to implement improvements in their own performance.

While the Virginia Department of Education encouraged school districts three years ago to begin to look at alternative assessments but gave no mandate, we helped initiate training on Performance-Based Assessments (PBAs) and rubrics, requiring Patrick County teachers to submit a minimum of one PBA each year.

Working alongside my team, the need to allow for data-driven instruction was apparent which led to the adoption of an adaptive intervention solution and Measures of Academic Progress (MAP) to measure student growth. The immediate feedback and built-in remediation, coupled with the actionable data, enabled Patrick County teachers to easily monitor student progress and differentiate their instruction.

Always looking to self-reflect, we collaborated with teachers to create a framework for structuring literacy time. Supporting the implementation of the Daily Five, a framework for structuring literacy time so students develop lifelong habits of reading, writing, and working independently, thus helping students develop independence, stamina, and accountability of their own reading development.

My hope was that by having teachers spend less time consumed by classroom management, they would be left with more for instruction and would be able to make it a priority. The framework has adapted flawlessly to our curriculum and state mandates and has improved school-wide literacy achievement.

Appreciating the idea of collaborating to improve student achievement, we helped foster a partnership with the Comprehensive Instructional Program (CIP). The CIP consortium is made up of more than 29 school divisions, designed to help instructors by providing lesson plans, activities, and assessments that are tightly aligned to the Virginia Standards of Learning in content and rigor. In my quest to stabilize the instructional program, additional supports were added to school-level instructional facilitators to help to build principals with the instructional program.

Guided by the belief that technology is a tool, and the need for instruction to drive technology to support new digital learning experiences, one of my first orders of business as superintendent was to establish a Bring Your Own Technology (BYOD) policy in schools, allowing devices to be used throughout classrooms.

Knowing the utilization of technology was imperative to our success, we set out to equip each teacher with a DVD player, document camera, new laptop and a teaching station. In each of the K-7 classrooms, an 84" Smart™ Kapp capture board was installed along with a Smart TV. Six laptops were given to each K-7 classroom across the division for center-based learning. In fact, we even launched a 1:1 Chromebook initiative at Patrick County High School in the 2017-2018 school year.

The increased technology has also led to an increased need for sufficient bandwidth; the district was successful in increasing their dedicated Internet access from 1GB to 2GB, raising our bandwidth to 743 kbps per student. With access to a Chromebook and the ability to connect via a wireless environment, students and teachers were able to actively participate in the consumption and production of media, build and contribute towards social networks, and be active participants in developing ideas that could be utilized to solve complex problems.

Realizing a need to revitalize classrooms and enhance learning spaces, rooms were painted and redesigned by staff. Alternative seating options were explored and facilitated in every building across the division to help plan focused and engaged learning experiences with a concentration on collaboration among individual students and among students and the teacher.

This learner-centered environment with various grouping formats has increased collaboration and communication in innovative learning spaces. These formats have included, but are not limited to peer-to-peer discussion, small-group work, student presentations, one-on-one instruction, and Socratic seminar. In this collaborative classroom, the teacher becomes a facilitator of learning while encouraging student growth, teamwork, critical thinking, and problem-solving skills.

With a free and reduced lunch rate at approximately 50% and limited access to extended learning opportunities in a rural location in Southwest Virginia, the ultimate goal is to level the playing field for all students. While the mind is being fed, so must the child, so we have ensured every child has access to a free breakfast.

After two years with a change in the instructional outlook, technology framework, and environmental factors in the classrooms, we became one of only 51 school districts fully accredited in the Commonwealth of Virginia.

A shared commitment to achieving improved results for children and working through challenging inequities of finance that impact instruction, I garnered the support from community stakeholders as co-investors and accountable partners in achieving to maneuver all the pieces of the puzzle to do what is best for students. The need to build local capacity and accountability was necessary to sustain improved results over time.

I still consistently attend community and school events promoting the use of timely, relevant and reliable data to share with stakeholders and ensuring accountability for each school and the district. I work with civic organizations within Patrick County, such as 4-H and Rotary, where I have spoken about my vision for public education

The goal is to continually improve student learning and foster a local, national and global perspective. This outreach has allowed critical thinking and self-reflection to implement best practices, bolster team leadership skills, and provide an opportunity to build capacity among the educators and parents.

I am an advocate of always seeking growth to benefit students, and have supported faculty members attending conferences across the Commonwealth of Virginia and asking each participant to come back and upload documentation for sharing in a Google Doc. These practices bring more rigor to the process of setting both short and long-term goals; ensure the wants, preferences, and needs of our community are well understood; and strategically focuses resources.

I encourage a professional growth mindset, which I believe is a vital component for a school district that is widely recognized as delivering outstanding education to students. Believing that education is primed for change in the Commonwealth, I also set up a viewing of the film Most Likely to Succeed to share with parents and community members what the future of education could and should look like for schools and students.

Financial burdens for the school division were overcome with forward thinking and a creative solution focused on providing the best resources for students in order to prepare them for the ever-changing workforce, higher- education, or military careers.

The truth is I could not have done any of the work I have done without the help of impactful teachers. I firmly believe whether you come from privilege, poverty, a great family or have a horrible upbringing, it is our responsibility to get to know our students at different levels, not only academically, but personally and socially. When teachers take advantage of opportunities to speak with their students about life outside of school, it is an indication to students that their teacher actually cares about them as a person. We all want to feel cared for and valued by the significant people in our world. Students are no different. In fact, students need this most often, no matter their status in the world.

There is no greater feeling as an educator than when a student, former or present, yells my name in a store or restaurant, comes up to me with a hug, introduces me to their significant other, bring their kid to me, or tells me about a new job. I still tell people who ask me that I am in the "kid business" and every chance I get, I go to schools and speak to students.

Last year, there was one student, in particular, I kept checking on. I had known Michael since he was an elementary student at Woolwine Elementary. He was a polite kid who was being raised by his grandmother. He would get into mischief sometimes when I was the principal so I got to know him fairly well.

Every time I saw him at the high school, I inquired about his grades.

A few years ago, I was invited to speak at the ROTC Banquet and was proud to see him as one of the leaders. At prom last year, I spoke with him as he came in and he told me everything was going well, but when he walked away the principal told me he was failing a class and graduation was in jeopardy.

I followed up a few days later with Michael when I went to the high school, and he told me he was going to fix it. I followed up again, and he still had not done his work and was behind. He had already delayed enlisting in the Marine Corp, and I decided to have the recruiter come out for a conference with Michael and me. He came out and we had a "come to Jesus" meeting with Michael about his future. He got the point, and the teacher, who rarely lets kids make up work in her class, allowed him to do so.

Michael graduated in May 2017 and left for boot camp a few months later.

One day, I hope I will see him again. I saw a lot of me in Michael. He struggled with his home life and with concentrating in school, and I knew the only way for him to be successful was to leave and have success on his own. I knew he could do it. I wanted it for him, and am glad I helped.

I have reported to Mrs. Bailey over the last 30 plus years because I wanted her to know I was successful because of her, and I have written this book to let everyone else know I am successful in spite of the obstacles.

It does take courage, but it also takes someone having a conversation with a young person letting them know they are not alone in this world.

Takeaways

So, nearly 20 years after I began this journey, aside from my children, this job has been the most rewarding thing I have ever done, and I know there are lessons I have learned and ones to learn in the future.

I think the first lesson to learn is that "You are what you say you are."

As an educator, I always tried my best to lift students up, instead of bringing them down. Do not get me wrong, I was a joker and we could kid around in my room, but in the end, I sought to relay to each student that they could do anything they wanted. I was honest. I told them they might have to sever friendships, take chances, and leave home. I told them that it may be uncomfortable, but it was worth it. I tell them that no one can define them, but themselves.

Be who they want to be. I explain to them the world is not easy but could be taken on by listening more than talking.

A lesson that many educators, at least the most successful ones, know is about building relationships and that the classroom cannot be the end of something for a student. I am not saying that you can reach out to every student and have an impact on his or her life, but what is the harm in trying?

When I left the sixth grade, Mrs. Bailey nor I realized the impact she had had on me then or how it would affect me later in life. What she did for me was not unusual; it was who she was as a person, and as an educator. The reaction for me was different than some, and I am sure the same for some. As an educator, I have tried to build relationships with students so they would know I cared about them and their success. Educators can be realistic with students when parents cannot reach them. They know how much time and effort was put into a test, project or homework and therefore should be honest in their feedback to students.

Educators should also be authentic with their students. Students know right away when adults are being fake or simply do not know what they are talking about. Being an educator is like no other job in the world. Human beings are counting on you so they can learn what the world has to offer. They come to you with some ideas and sometimes it is your job to introduce them to new information and sometimes it is your job to mold what they already know and help them understand how the information fits into the world.

In the last teaching position I held, I taught eighth grade civics and one point I would always try and make when we talked about the Committee of Five of the Second Continental Congress, was the state of mind of the representatives. We talked about everything from them being apart from their loved ones to the weather because it all factored in.

The point is teaching is about digging deep. It is about the learning; it is not about the assessments. I would tell my students' every day that civics was the most important class they would take in the eighth grade and I believed it.

Teachers work tireless hours and are tired when they go home, but I can tell you showing up at extra curricula activities of your students will go a long way. It will not matter if it is a play, a game, a club, or simply an after-school activity. It does not mean you have to go every week or even stay the entire time, but I can tell you your presence will not go unnoticed.

Part of my success as a teacher was to make sure my students knew that emotions matter. I would use them to prime the pump for learning, to inspire self- direction, and to recognize each student full as a human being. Often teachers have to challenge themselves not to react personally to certain emotions that may seem antagonizing or otherwise problematic, but rather to focus on students feeling not just heard, but fully understood as human beings with complex histories and circumstances that color their learning experiences no matter how clinical you try to make them.

Mrs. Bailey allowed this into her room. Mr. Beason did this for me, as well, which gave me the courage to change my name.

One of the biggest misses for new teachers is to not trust their students. Trusting a student communicates more than you can otherwise put into words. Give them chances to see the value and complexity of trust. This is a life lesson.

The last thing I can offer as advice is to pay attention. Recognizing the nuances of each student—their patterns, their insecurities, the fact that they wear two different shoes because they think it looks cool—proves to them that you see them as people, not students. This also helps to recognize if there are any problems, issues at home, bullying at school or anything else that can affect their lives.

Retrospect

My brother used to say, "I'm going to write a book and it's going to be called, 'You won't believe this shit.'"

It has taken me years to decide to finally write this book. I was embarrassed by most of the events in my life and was scared about the outcome. But now I realize sharing my story may help some who have gone through similar circumstances to heal. I could sit around and complain about what happened, but where will that get me?

All I can do about the past is learn from it, and I have.

The lessons have been hard ones. I am in no way living the perfect life, but I have been granted the opportunity to make a difference.

I have loved deeply. I have served my country with honor, and have been able to work in the greatest profession I could imagine. I am grateful for the people I have met on this journey, and I cannot wait for the years I have left so I can hopefully make an impact on the world like Mrs. Bailey made on mine.

Maybe it is one, maybe it is many, but everyone needs at least one person who believes in them—who sees them for who they are and who still cares. It does not mean it changes everything. Bad stuff happens, good stuff happens, and life still rolls around. It is what the individual does with it that matters, but we can have an impact.

The great educator Rita Pierson said, "Every child deserves a champion—an adult who will never give up on them, who understands the power of connection and insists that they become the best they can possibly be."

Mrs. Bailey was my champion and remains my champion. I am grateful she touched my life, so all the other things that happened do not matter. I had the courage to move past them.

I know I have lived this life the best I could and have made my way the best I can. Have I done it well? Sometimes I think so; sometimes I think I could do better. I think everyone does. It is not about all these events that happen; it is about how I pushed past them. You cannot constantly look back. The past cannot be changed, but your perspective of it can.

I could easily have lived a life full of hate but in the words of Martin Luther King, Jr., "I have decided to stick with love. Hate is too great a burden to bear."

Dr. William D. Sroufe is an award-winning educator and division superintendent in the Commonwealth of Virginia. In addition to his work in education, Dr. Sroufe has written two books of poetry: *Words from a Journal* (2014) and *Starting a Conversation: Poems and Prose* (2017) both by Akmaeon Publishing. A former U.S. Air Force journalist, he has also done feature writing for *Airman Magazine*, *The Pilot*, and *The Roanoke Times*. Dr. Sroufe has a Doctorate in Education with a major in Educational Leadership. He has taught eighth through twelfth grade physical science, world geography, information technology and civics in Virginia.

Rachelle Chartrand is an award-winning screenwriter, producer, and author. In addition to her extensive work in film and TV, in September 2014, she released her memoir, *CHRYSALIS: A Dark and Delicious Diary of Emergence* and has since ghostwritten or co-written four others. Rachelle has a Bachelor of Secondary Education with a major in physics and a minor in math, but has an eclectic teaching resume, having taught students of all ages and backgrounds around the world, including young offenders and at-risk youth at an independent school in Vancouver, BC.

CPSIA information can be obtained
at www.ICGtesting.com
Printed in the USA
BVHW09s1712280718
522786BV00006B/22/P